GOD IS COOL

by Liam Nolan

Awaken your clown chakra

For more information, contact
Ananda Gurukula Publications
P.O. Box 9655
Santa Rosa, CA. 95405

liamscreations.com

©2017 Liam Nolan
All Rights Reserved

ISBN 978-0-692-93984-0
Revised edition 2017

Many thanks to Kalle Kannisto, Lisa Flora,
Jugney and my dear wife Maetreyii
for all of their help in putting
this book together.

Why did God create the Universe?

...He just needed a little space.

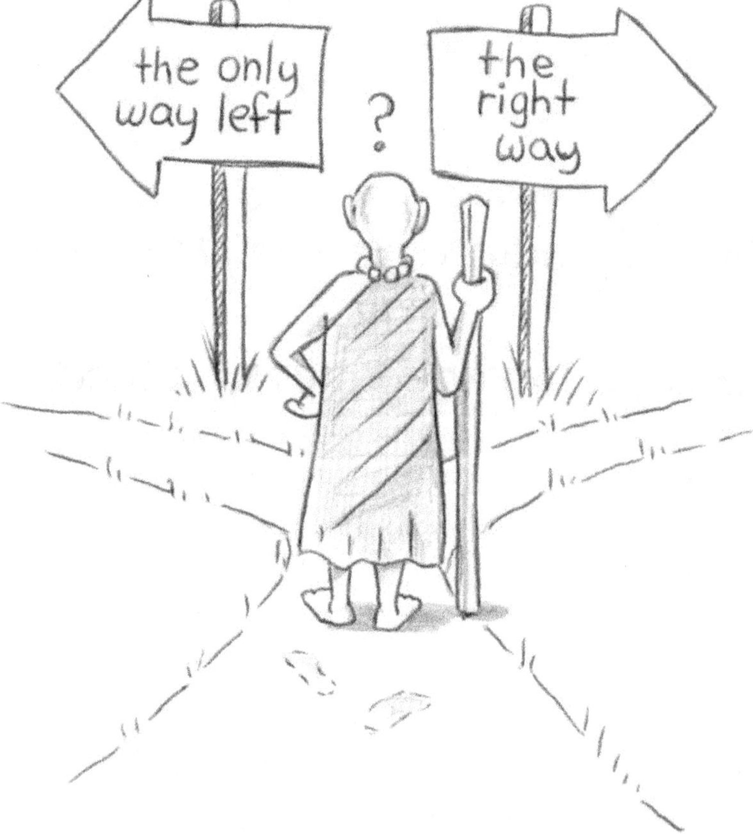
the only way left
the right way
?

wherever I go
so does my E go

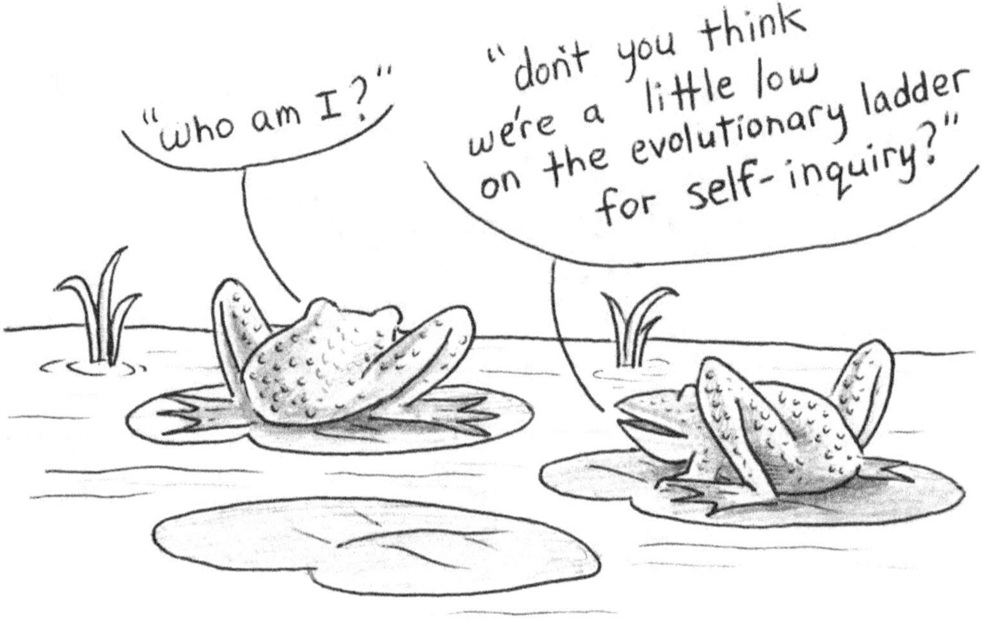
"who am I?"
"don't you think we're a little low on the evolutionary ladder for self-inquiry?"

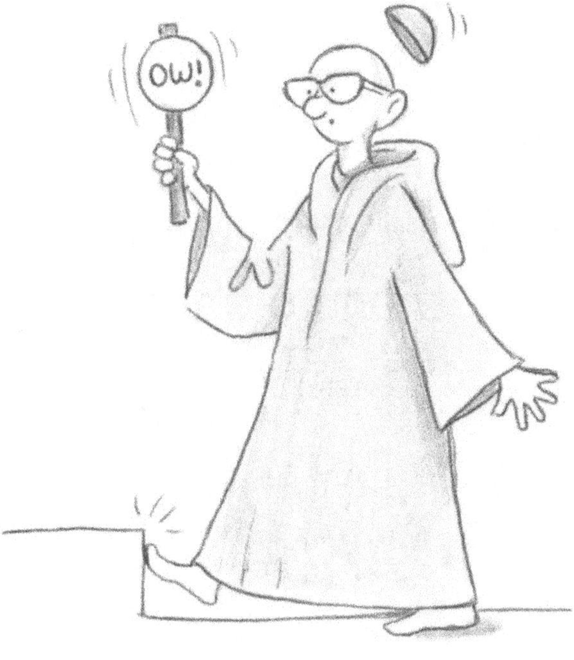
OW!

a silent monk stubs his toe

I'm more humble
than you are

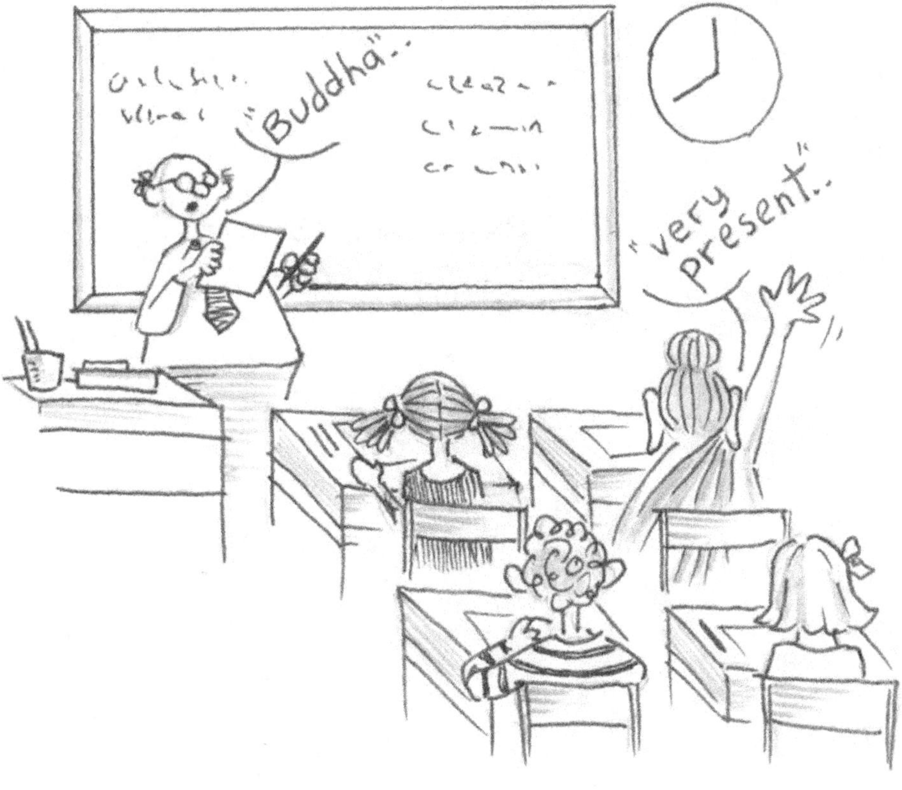
"Buddha"..
"very present"..

everything is
relative

even your
relatives

self-reflection

nothing is permanent
even a permanent

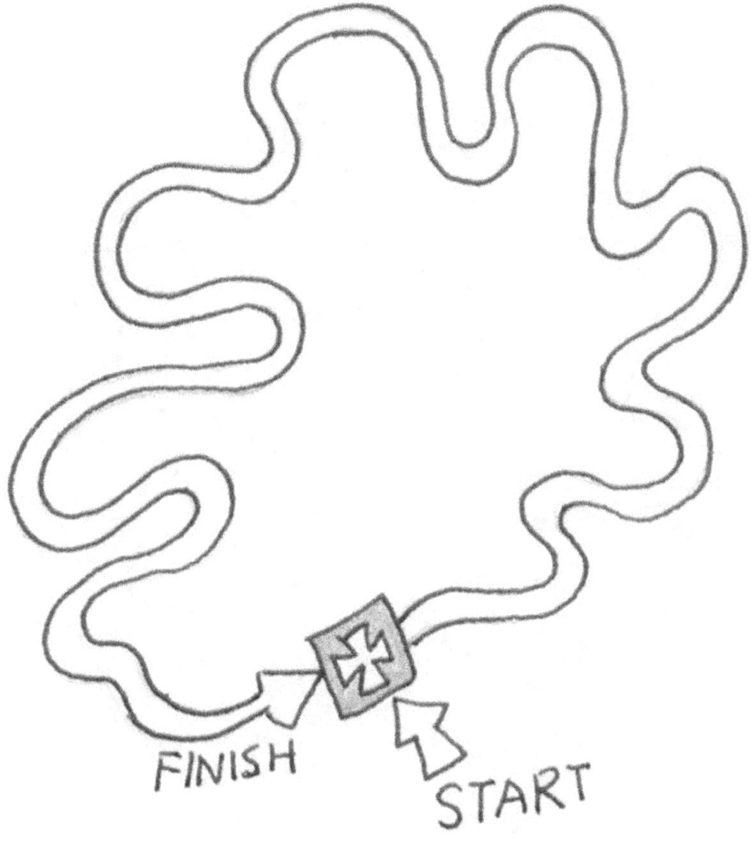
FINISH
START

aerial view of
the road to enlightenment

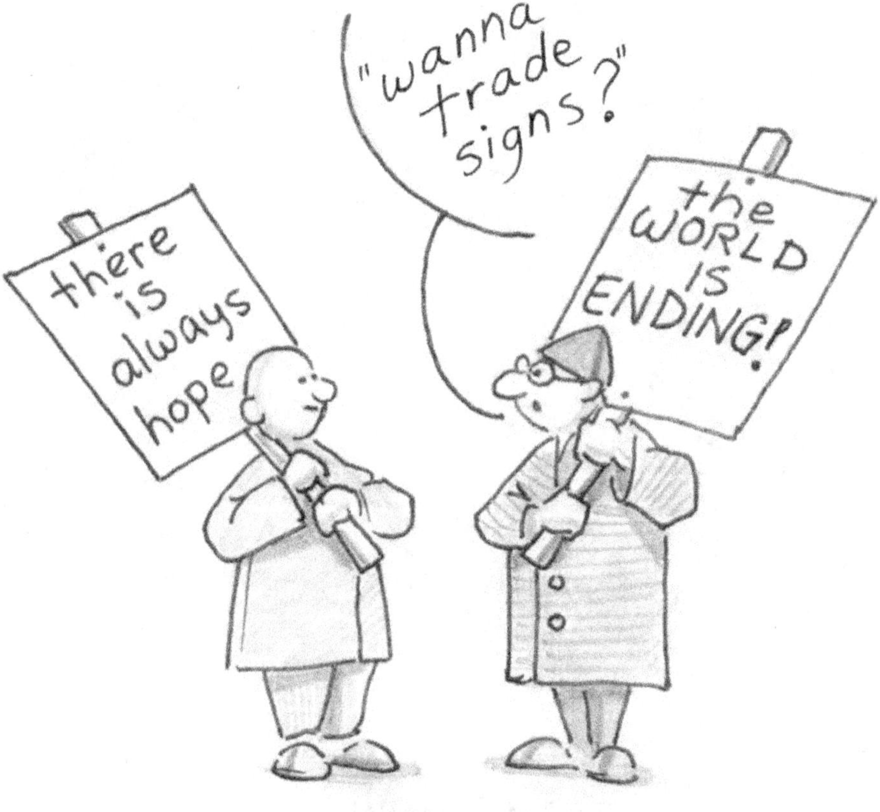
there is always hope
"wanna trade signs?"
the WORLD IS ENDING!

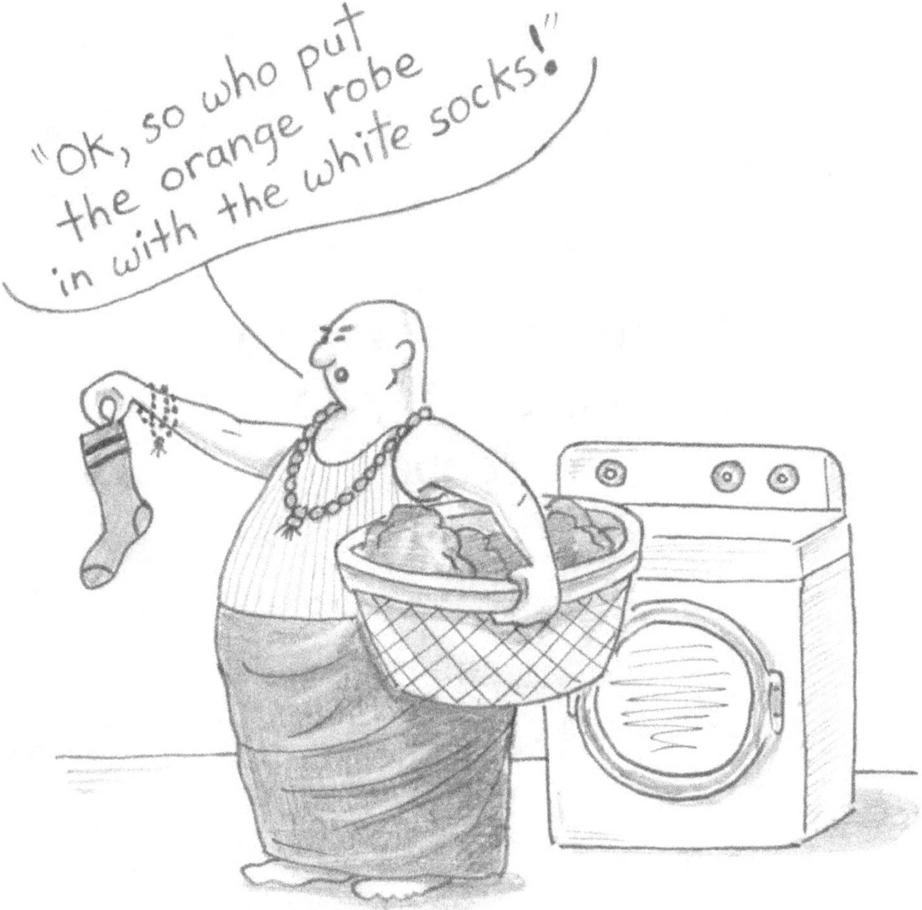
"OK, so who put the orange robe in with the white socks!"

daily life in the monastery

No matter how many
times I try to
escape

I'm still free

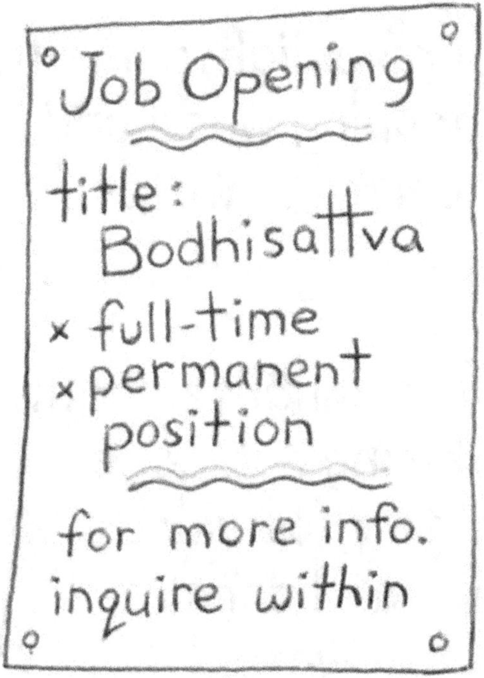
Job Opening
title: Bodhisattva
× full-time
× permanent position
for more info. inquire within

Before enlightenment,
chopping wood and
carrying water

After enlightenment,
hiring someone
to chop wood
and carry
water

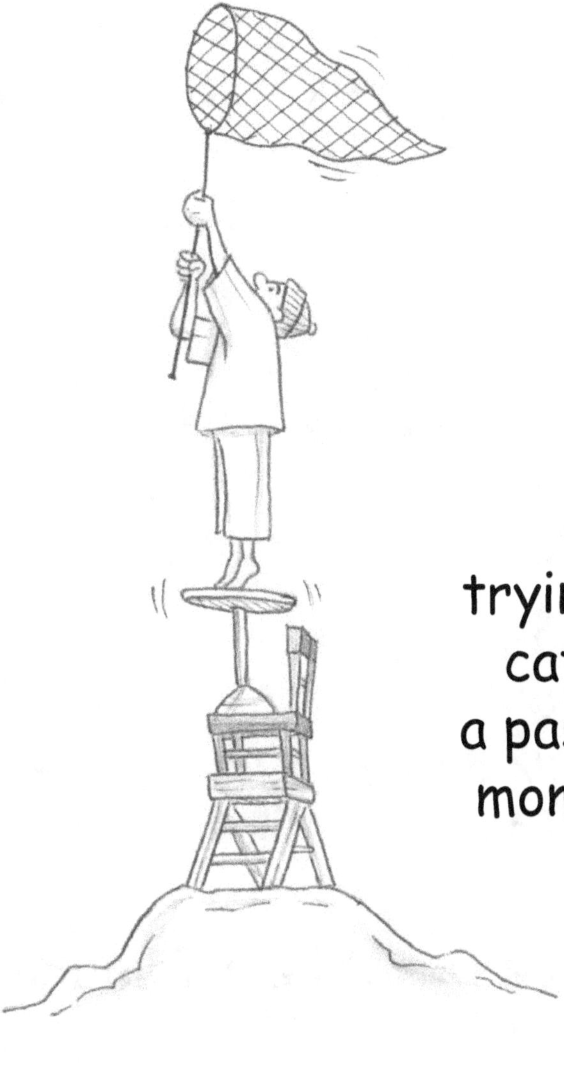

trying to
catch
a passing
moment

the Great Pear Buddha

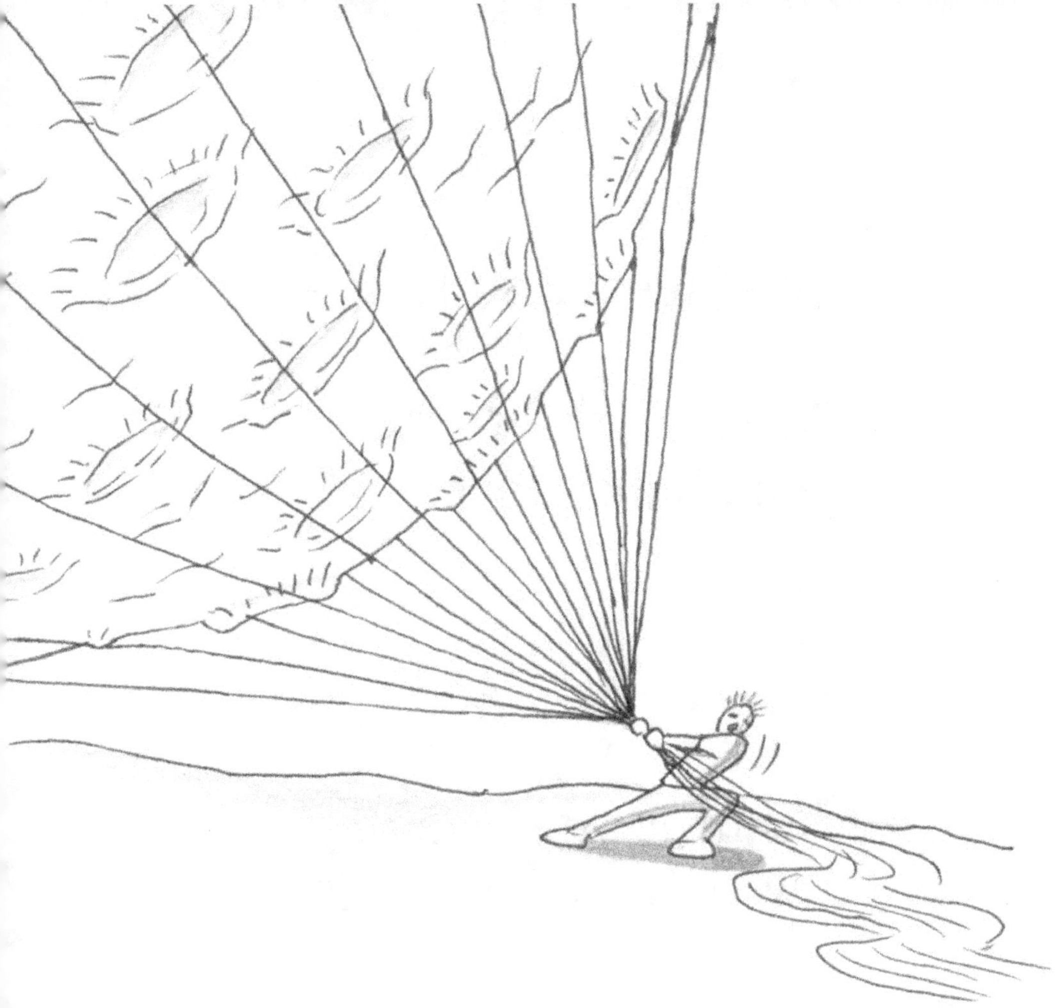

just let go

first level Zen Koan -

"what is the sound of one hand clapping?"

second level Zen Koan -

"what is the sound of two hands clapping?"

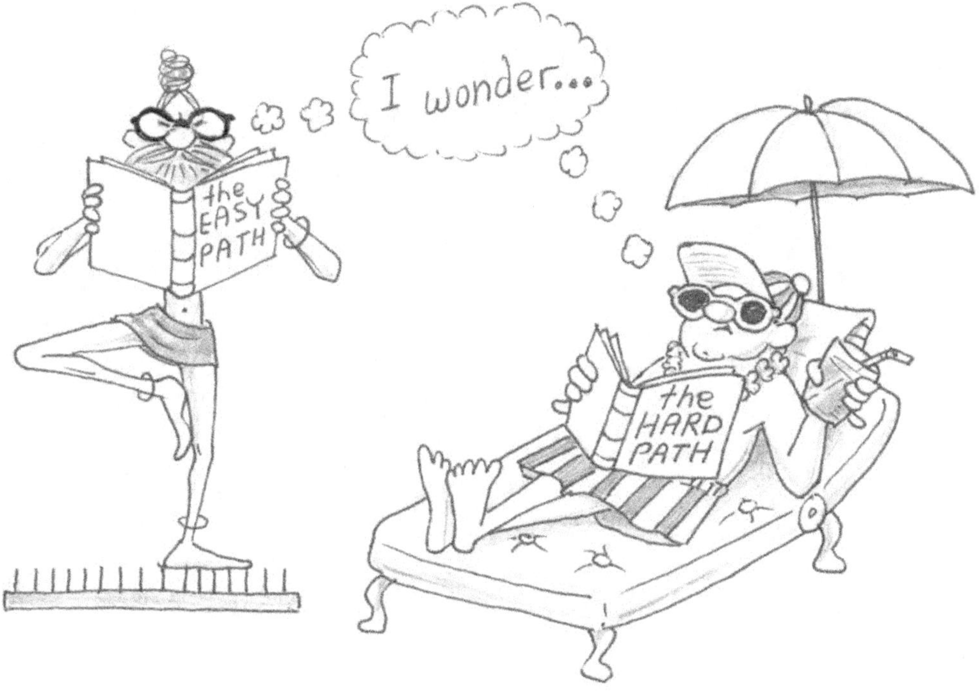
I wonder...
the EASY PATH
the HARD PATH

never satisfied

ring
I was expecting your call...
I know...
I knew you knew that...
I knew you knew that I knew that...
I sense you're about to wish me a nice day...
Yes.. have a nice day, though I already know you'll have a nice day...
I know...
click!

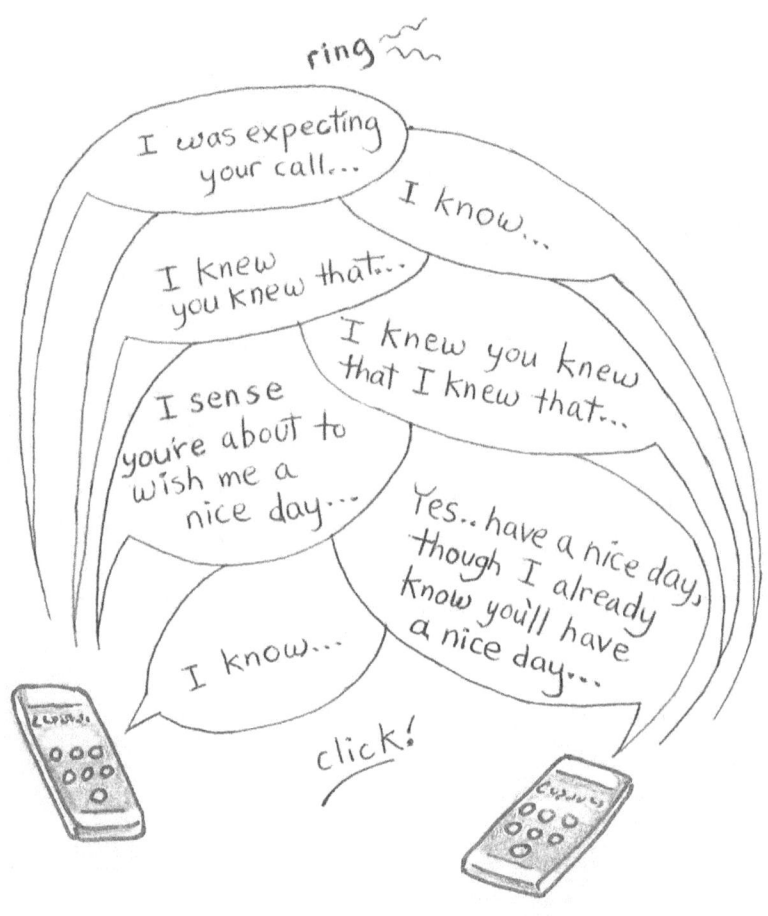

Psychic readers talking to each other

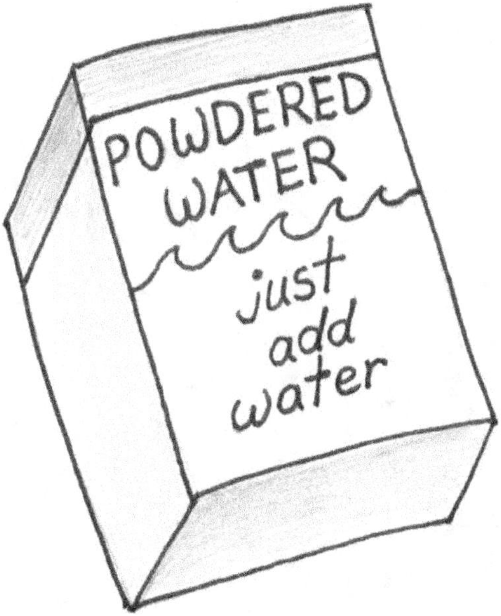
POWDERED
WATER
just
add
water

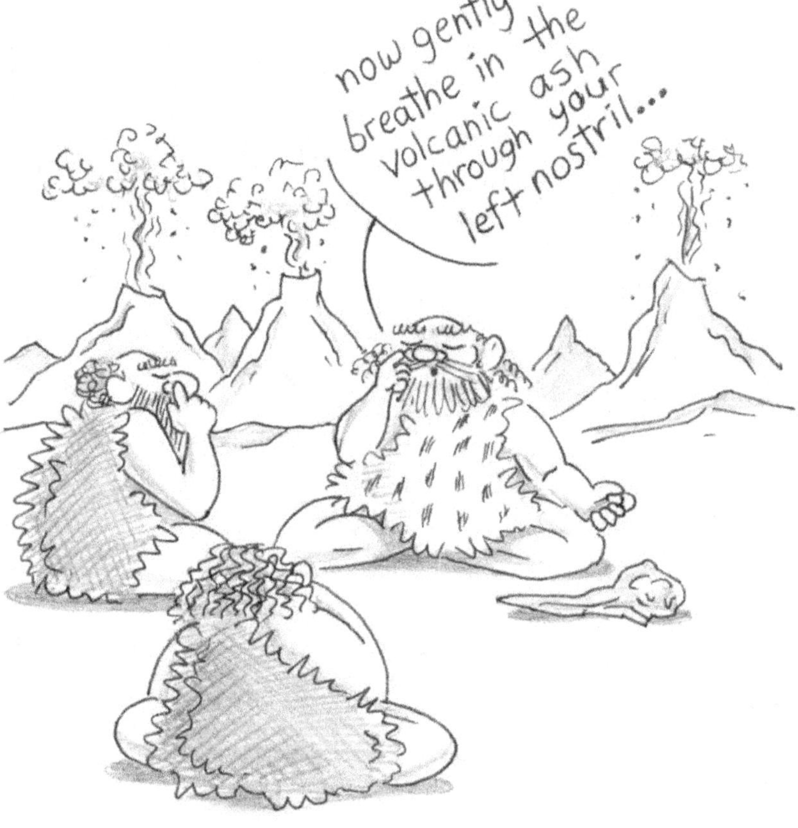
now gently breathe in the volcanic ash through your left nostril...

the first meditation class

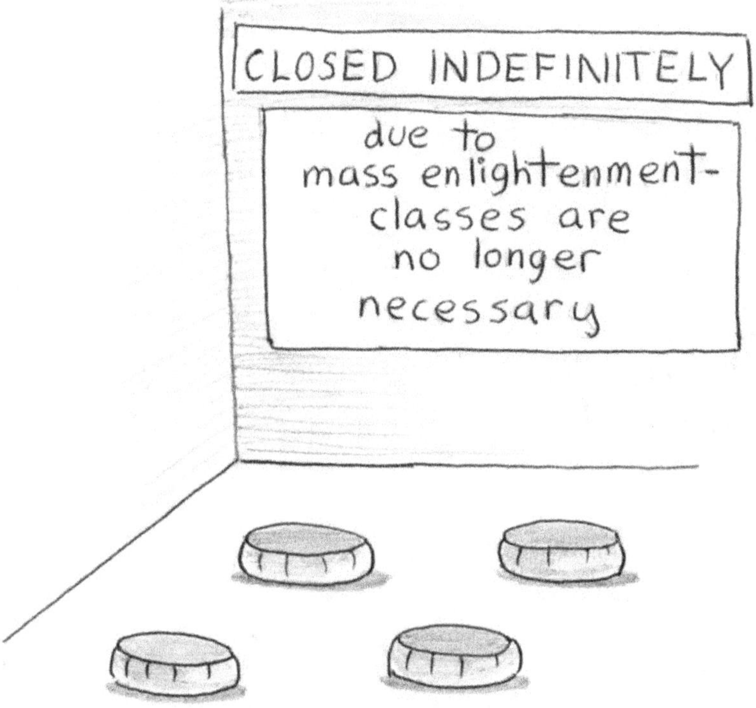
CLOSED INDEFINITELY
due to
mass enlightenment-
classes are
no longer
necessary

meditation class
in the far far future

I would like to procrastinate
but I keep putting it off.

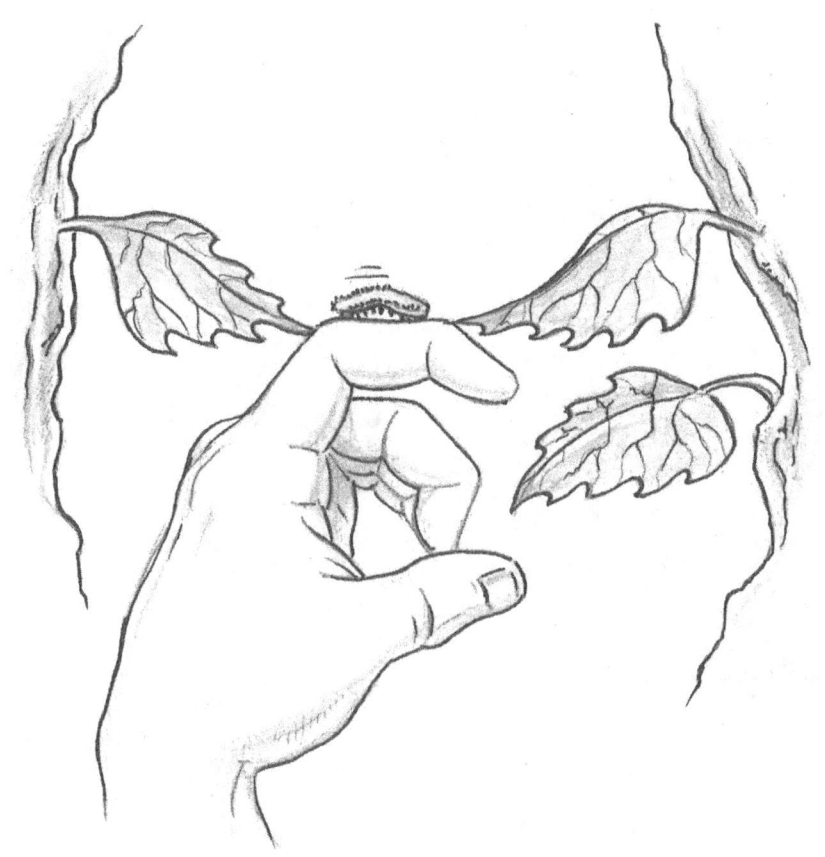

there's always someone who needs a hand

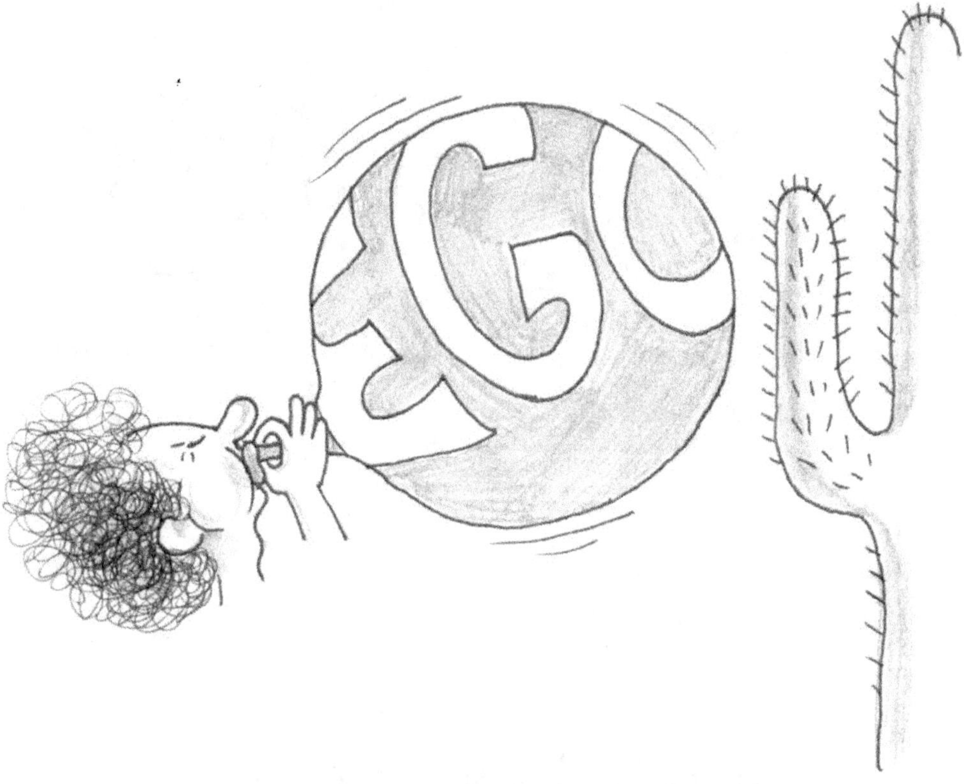
EGO

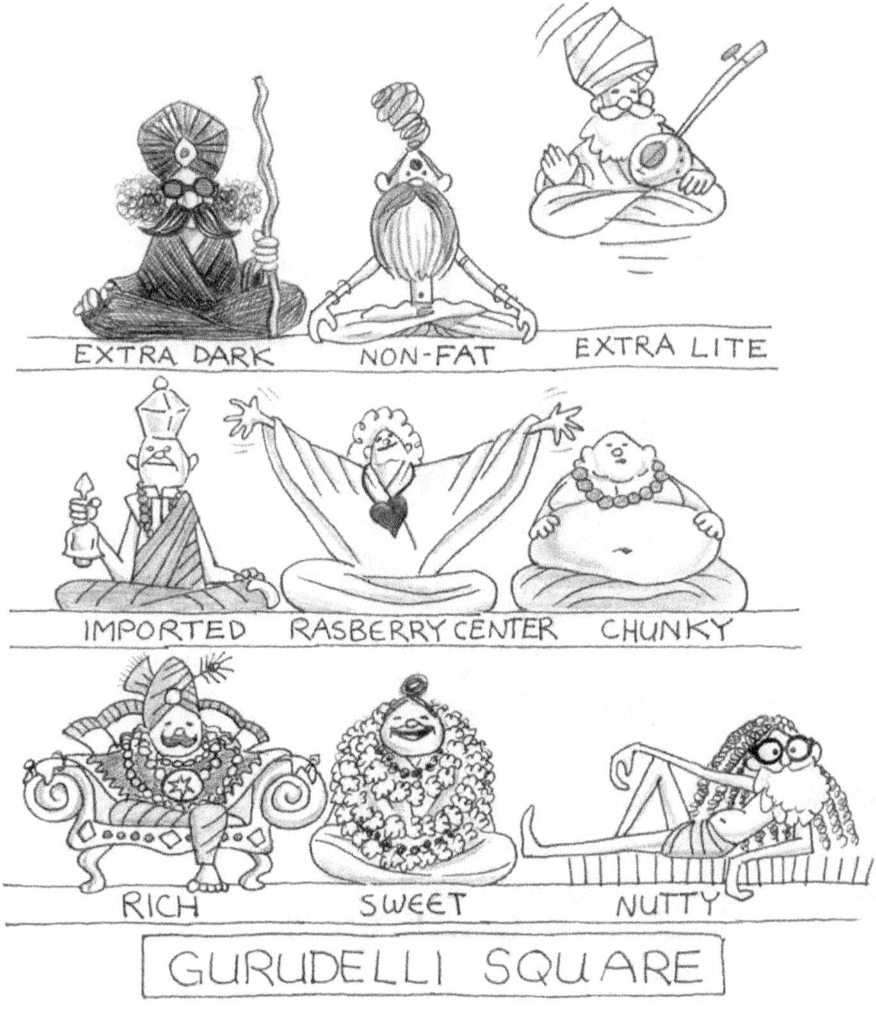
EXTRA DARK
NON-FAT
EXTRA LITE
IMPORTED
RASBERRY CENTER
CHUNKY
RICH
SWEET
NUTTY
GURUDELLI SQUARE

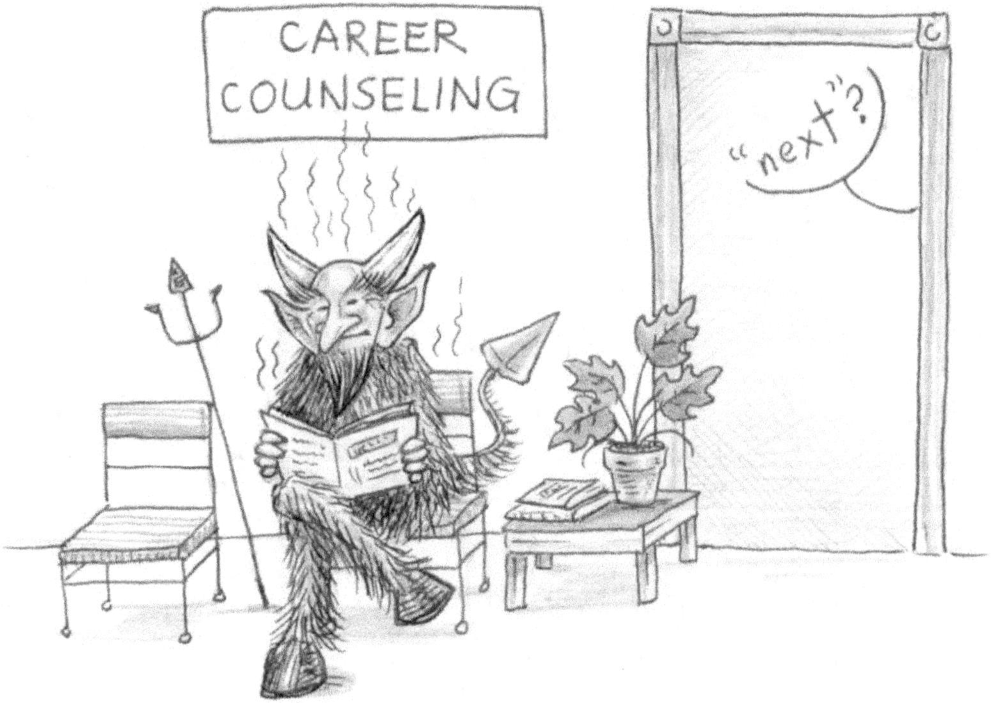
CAREER COUNSELING
"next"?

Job burnout

Be is for Buddha

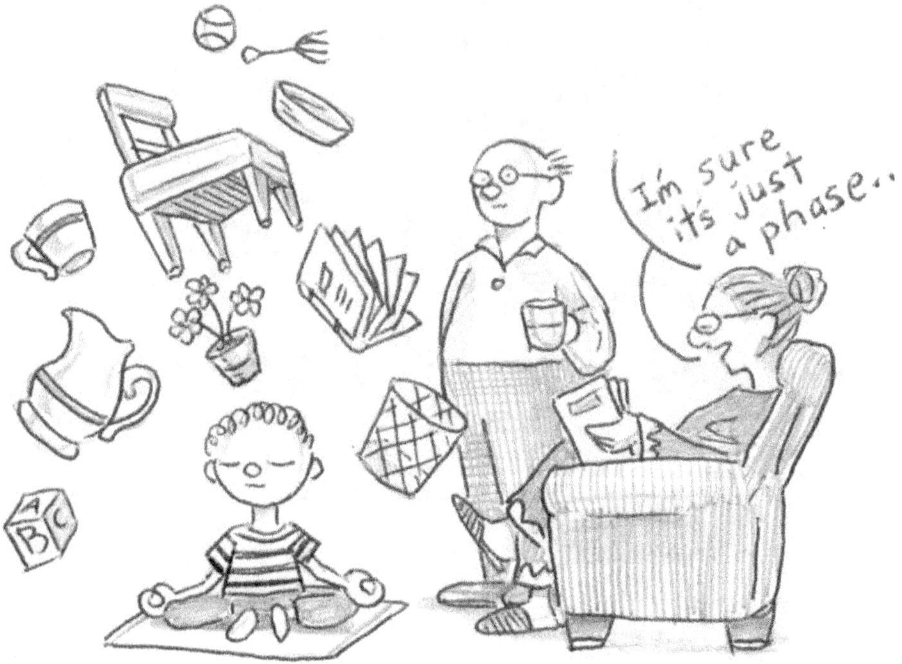
I'm sure it's just a phase..

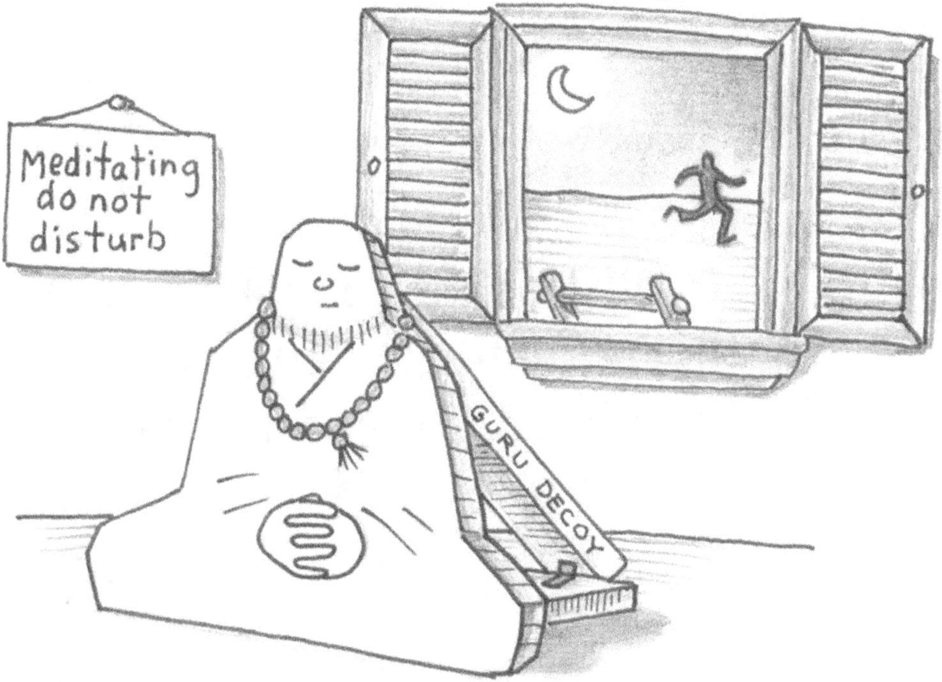
Meditating do not disturb
GURU DECOY

Guru's secret night out

If all this is a dream,
then I really wonder what
God ate before going to bed.

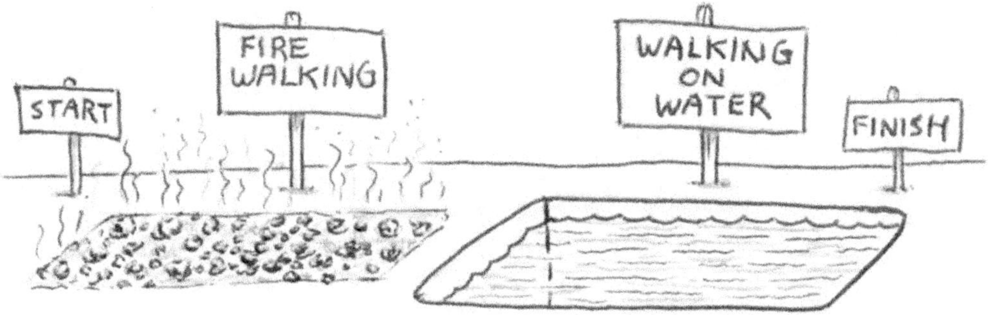
START
FIRE WALKING
WALKING ON WATER
FINISH

this is a human... being

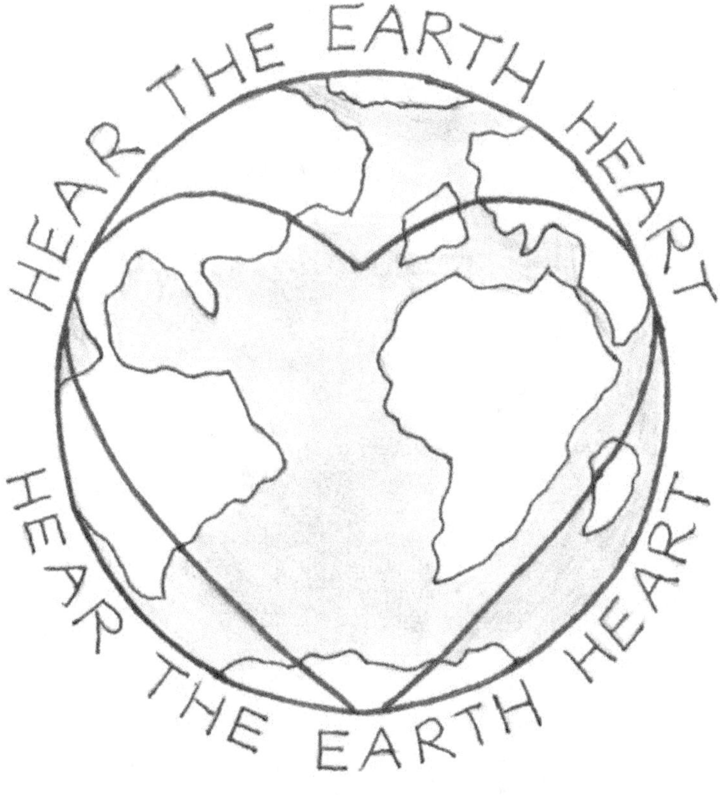
HEAR THE EARTH HEART
HEAR THE EARTH HEART

EARTHEARTHEARTH
HEARTHEARTHEART

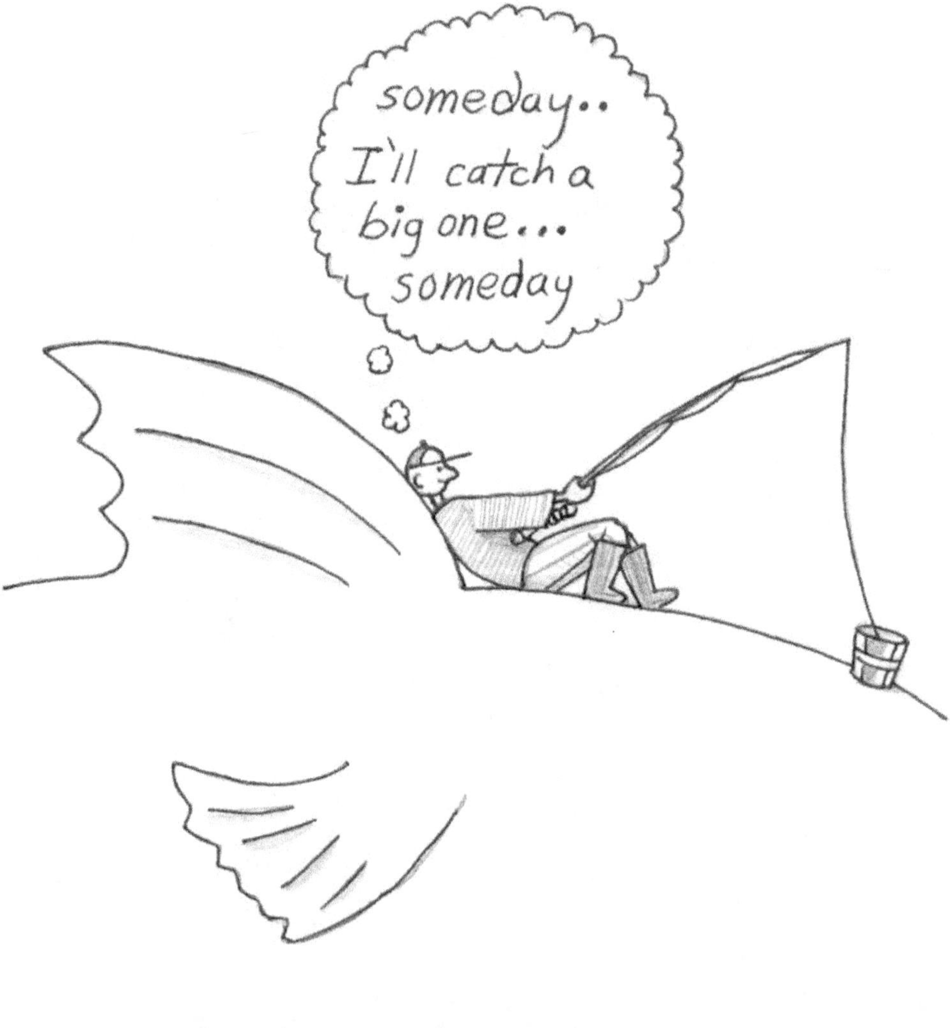
someday.. I'll catch a big one... someday

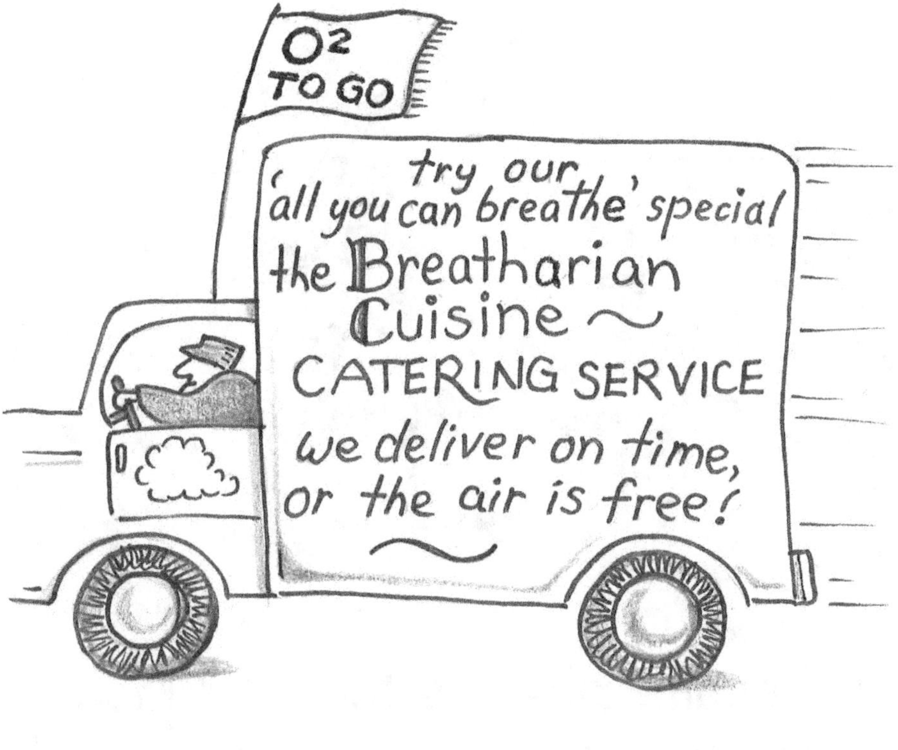
O2
TO GO
try our
'all you can breathe' special
the Breatharian
Cuisine ~
CATERING SERVICE
we deliver on time,
or the air is free!

it became obvious that the monks were uneasy with the new arrival

somewhere in there
is your true face

"Please pass the peace"

HALOS
HORNS
HEADPHONES

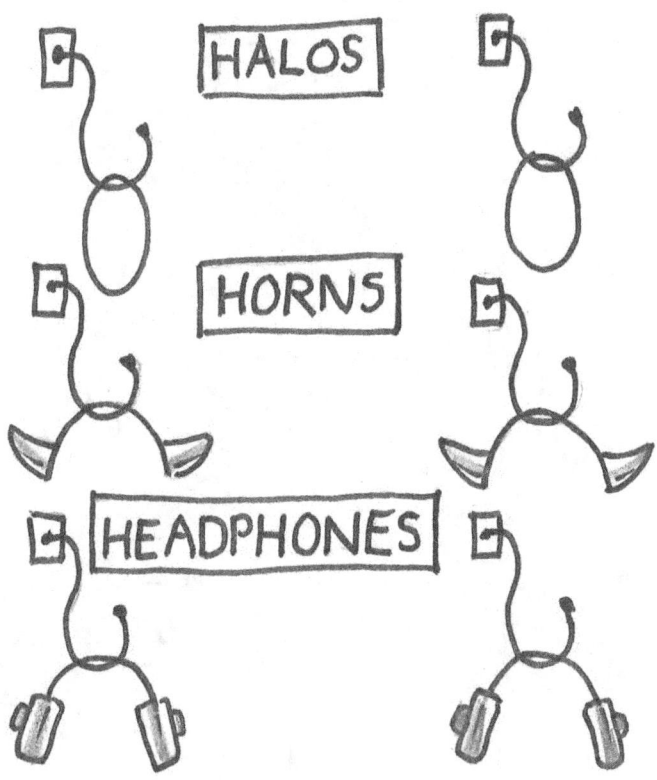

so many choices

Global Cooling

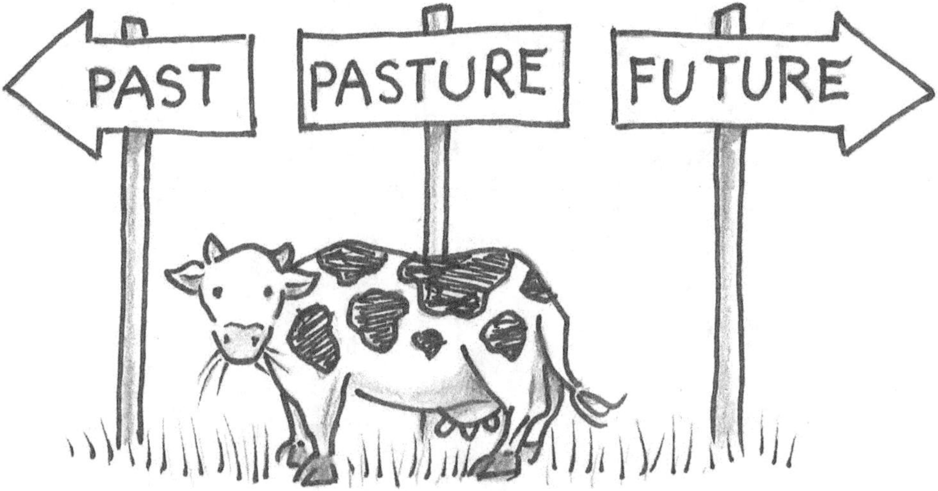
PAST
PASTURE
FUTURE

cow in the now

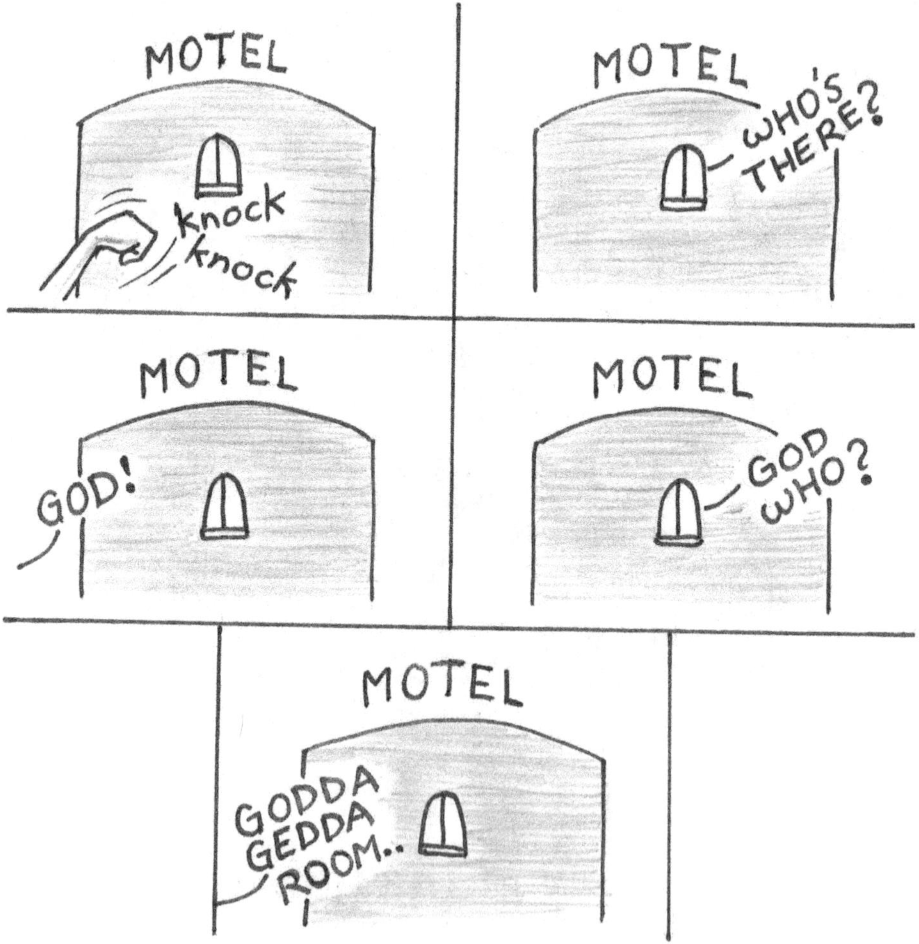
MOTEL
knock
knock
MOTEL
WHO'S THERE?
MOTEL
GOD!
MOTEL
GOD WHO?
MOTEL
GODDA GEDDA ROOM..

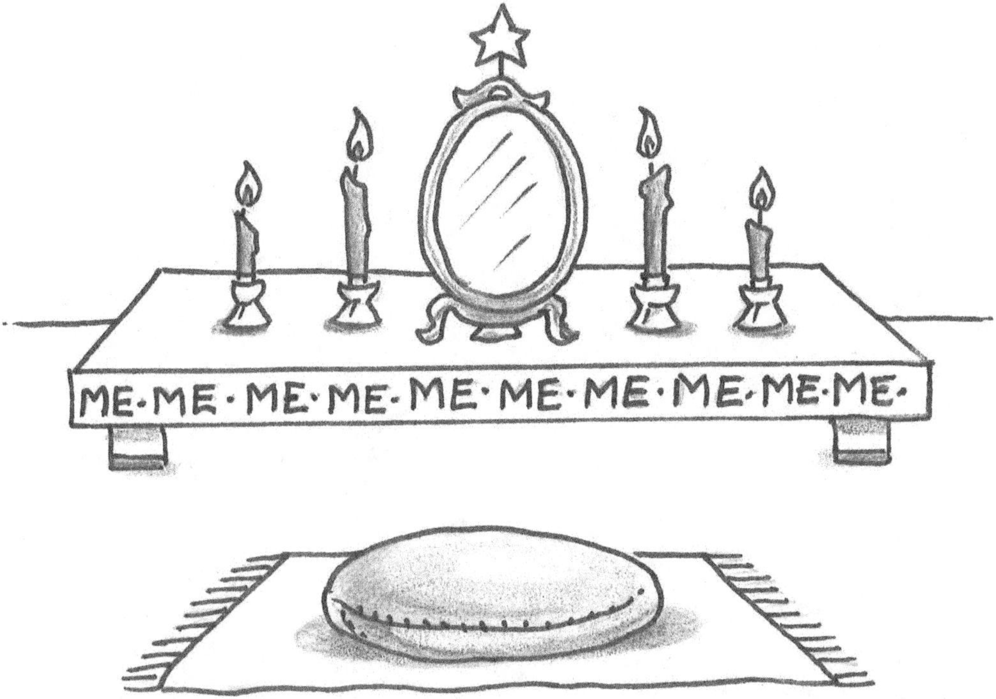
ME·ME·ME·ME·ME·ME·ME·ME·ME·ME·

altar ego

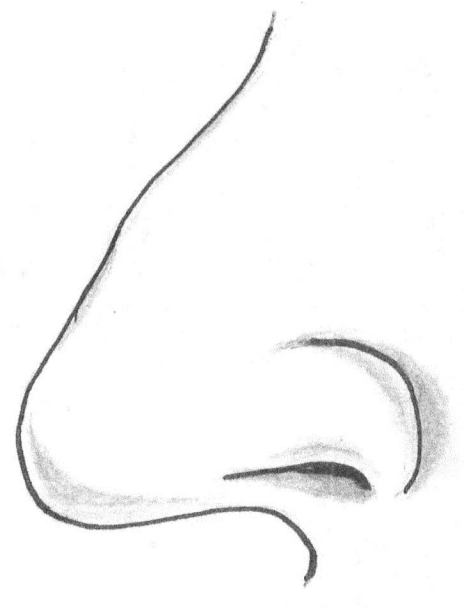

BEHOLD! The all-smelling nose

the only sign on the spiritual path

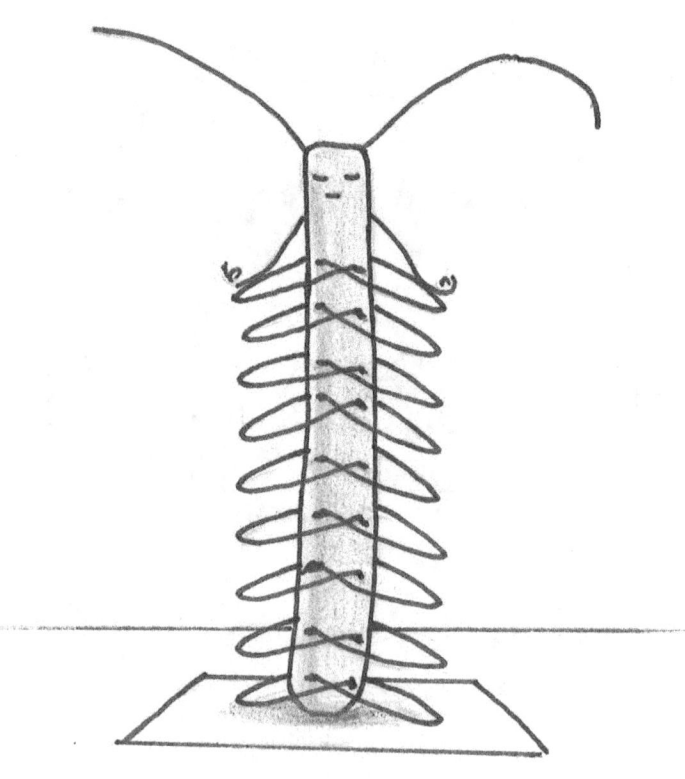

centipede yogi

a no-thought bubble

Buddha's first words
after enlightenment....

"I am awake,
but my foot is asleep"

Future Life Readings
100% correct or your Money Back!

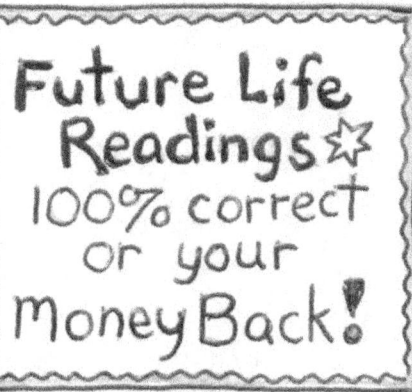

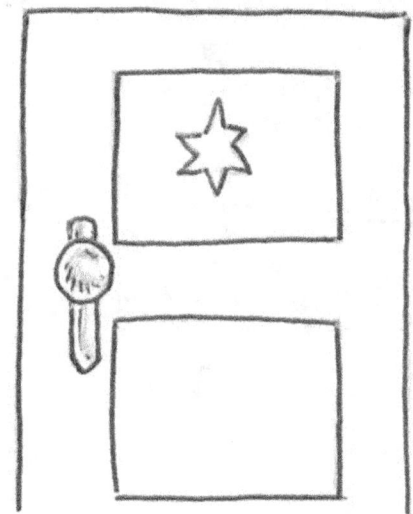

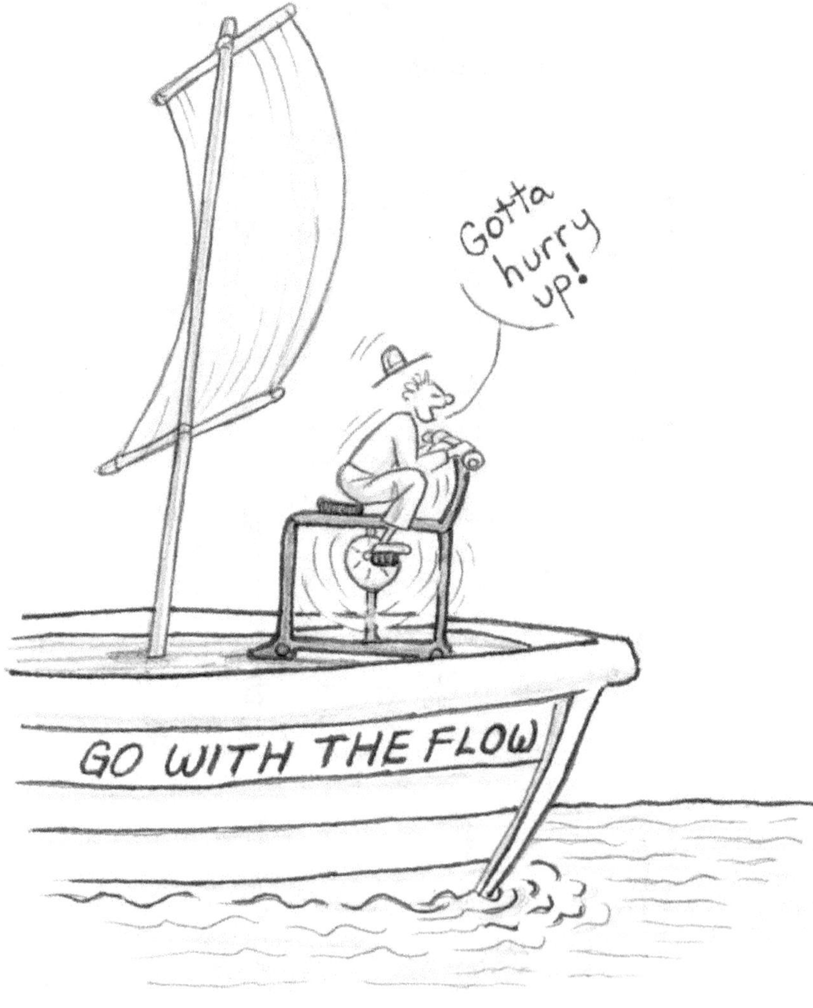
Gotta hurry up!
GO WITH THE FLOW

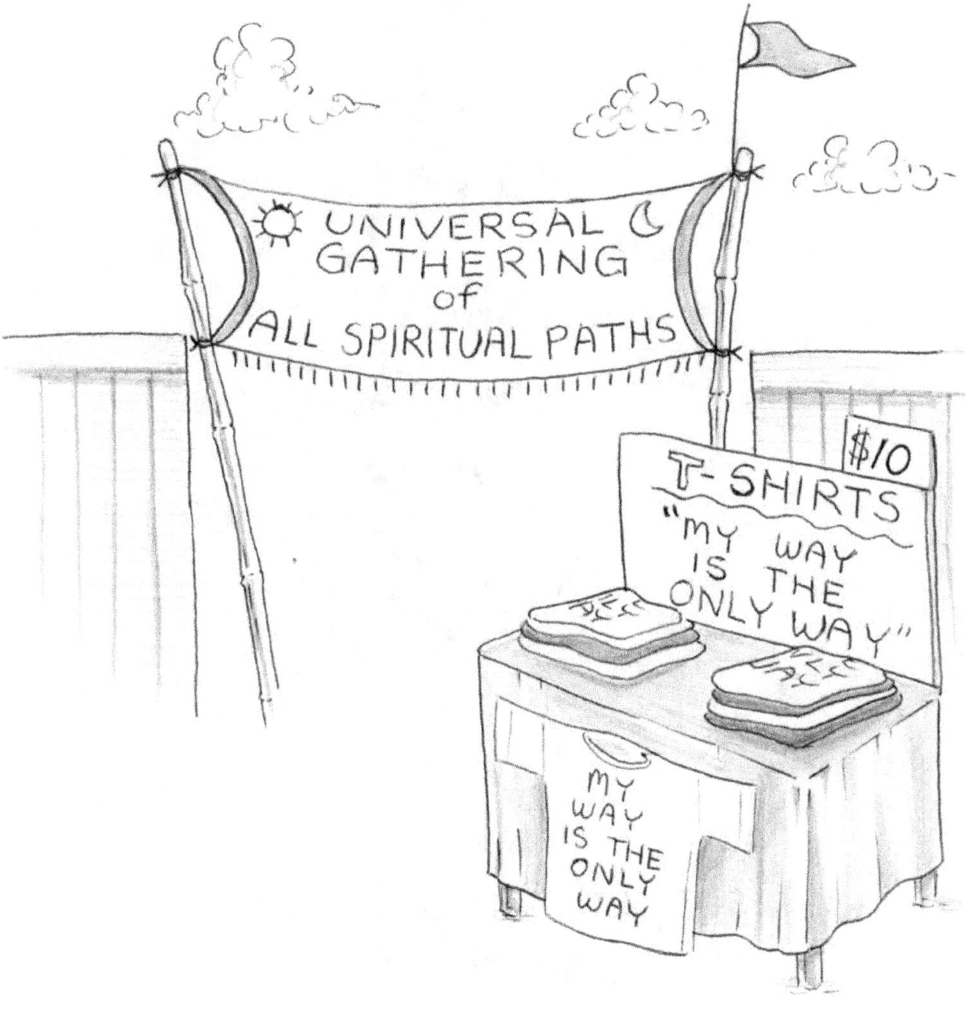
UNIVERSAL
GATHERING
of
ALL SPIRITUAL PATHS
$10
T-SHIRTS
"MY WAY
IS THE
ONLY WAY"
MY
WAY
IS THE
ONLY
WAY

Ganesh slipped through the crowd...
unnoticed

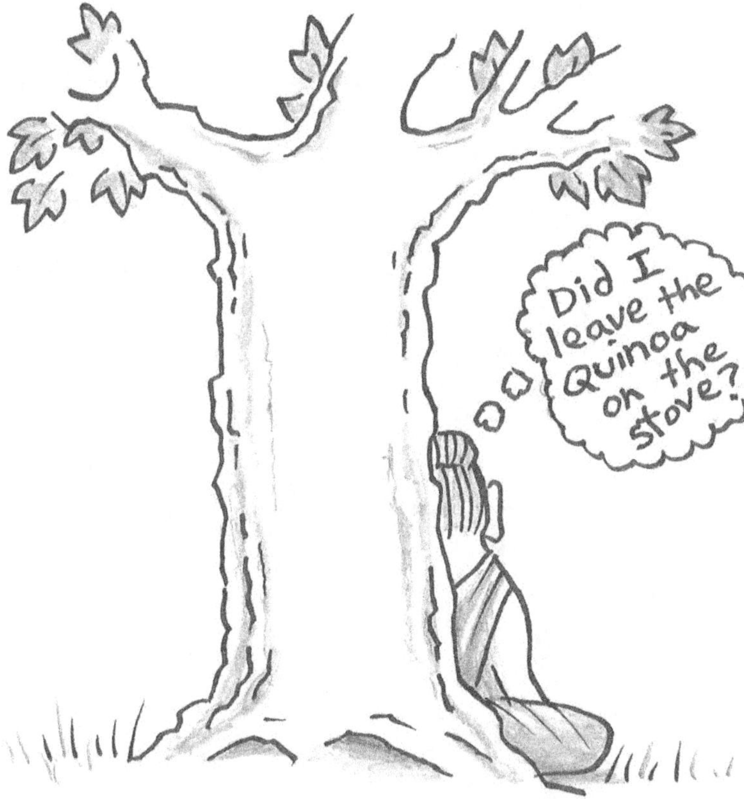
Did I leave the Quinoa on the stove?

Buddha's last thought
before enlightenment

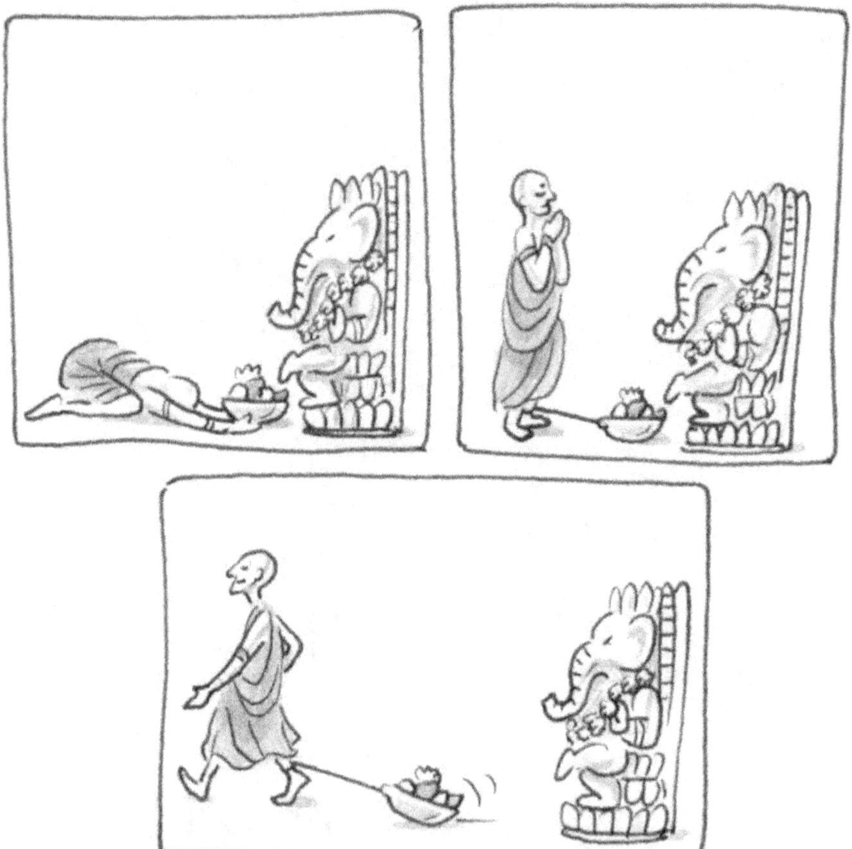

I will live in the
here and now

in a few minutes

May you be opened
by the
Christmas
presence

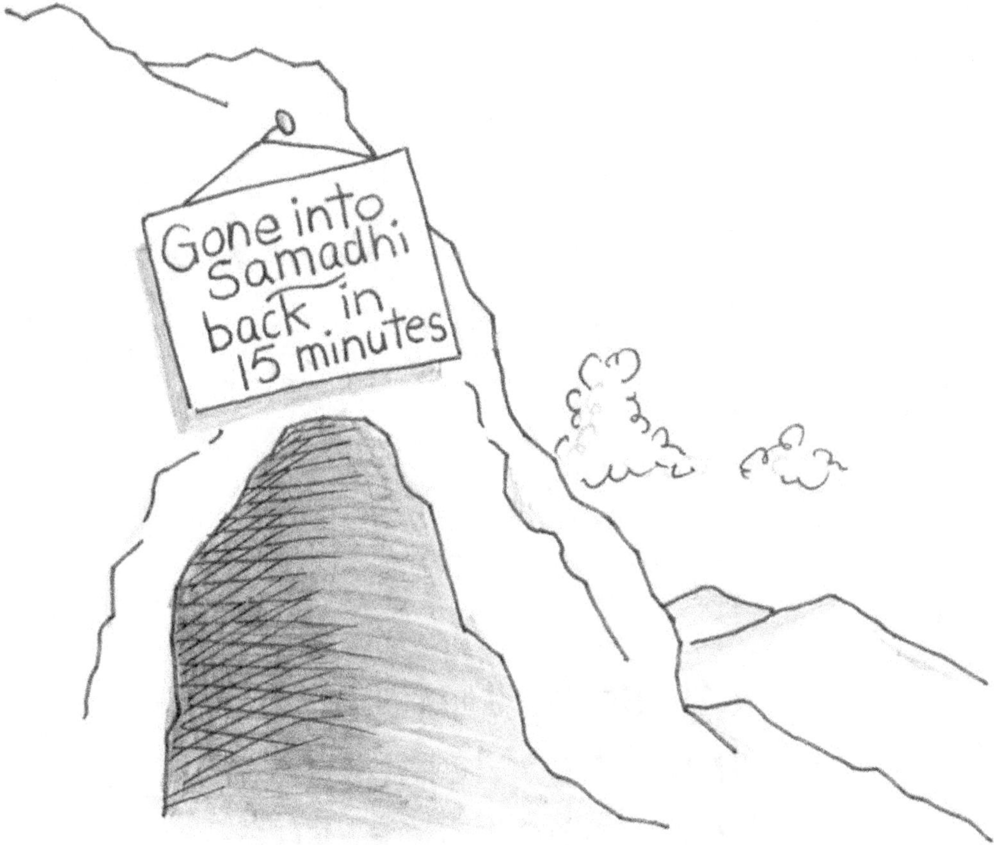
Gone into
Samadhi
back in
15 minutes

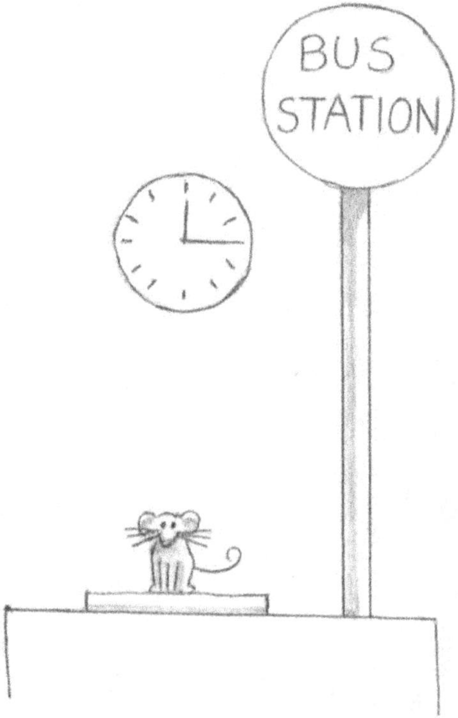
BUS
STATION

both saint and sinner
should contemplate
that if the bus is late
we all must wait

PRIMITIVE LEVITATION DEVICE OF THE HUMANS

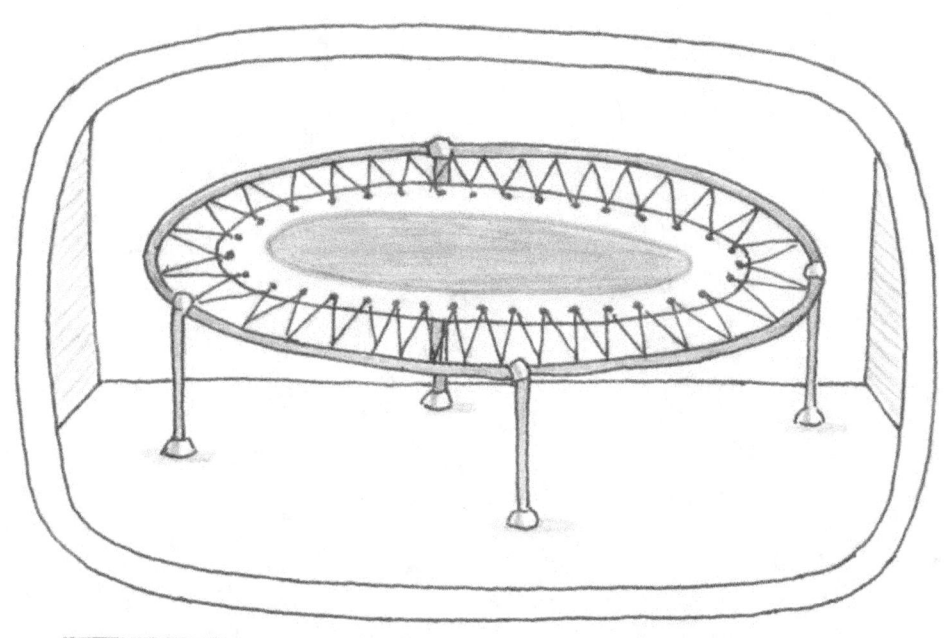

Museum
year - 10,000 A.D.

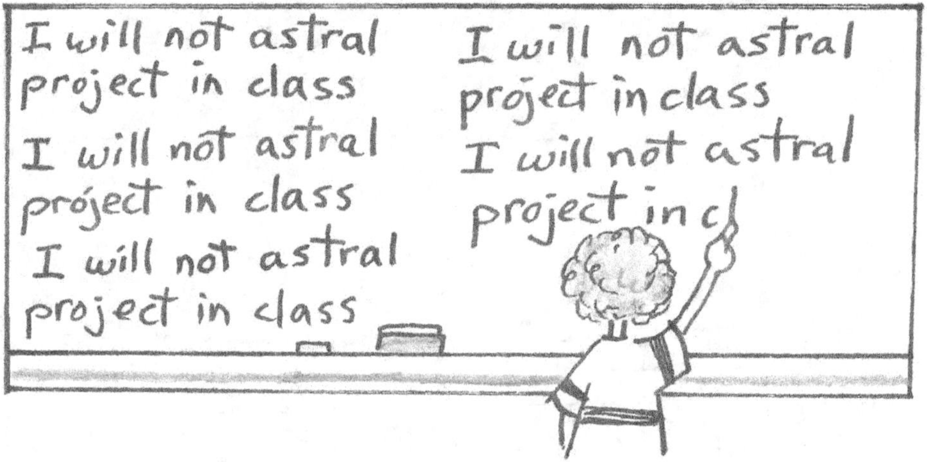
I will not astral
project in class
I will not astral
project in class
I will not astral
project in class
I will not astral
project in class
I will not astral
project in cl

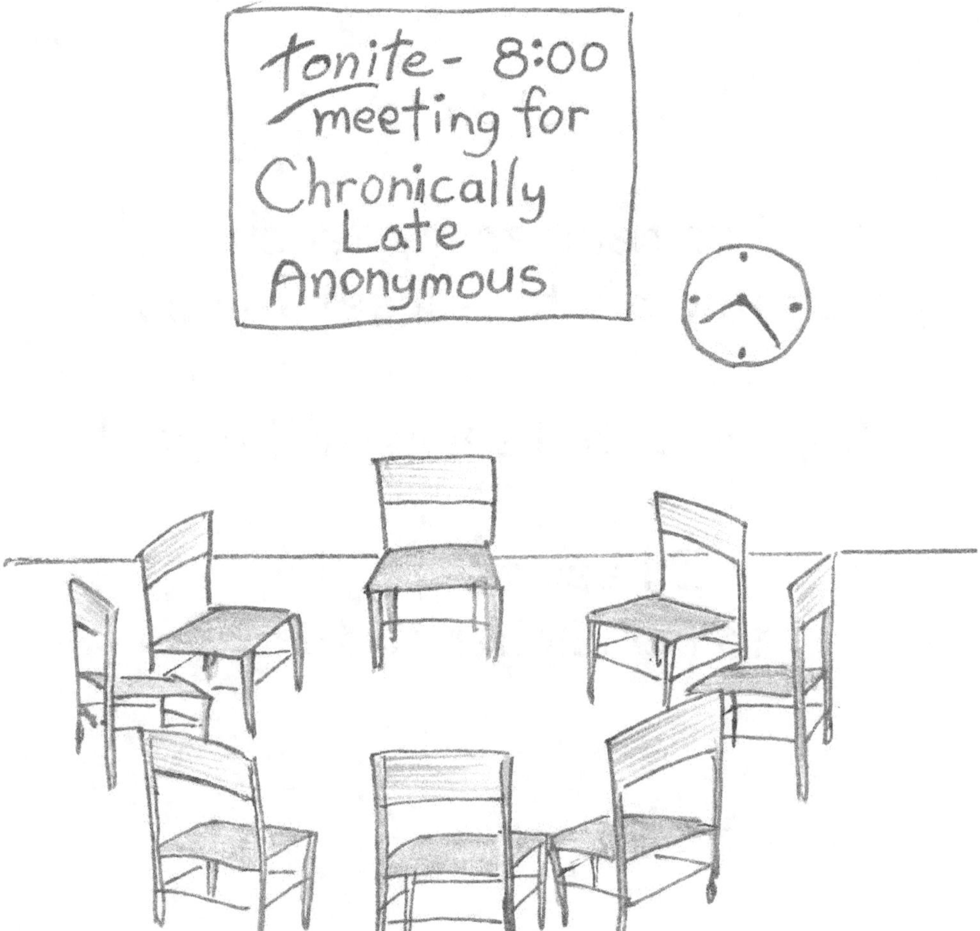
tonite - 8:00
meeting for
Chronically
Late
Anonymous

I remember my teacher once told me to "forget the past."

So, since that's now in the past,

I keep forgetting to remember to forget

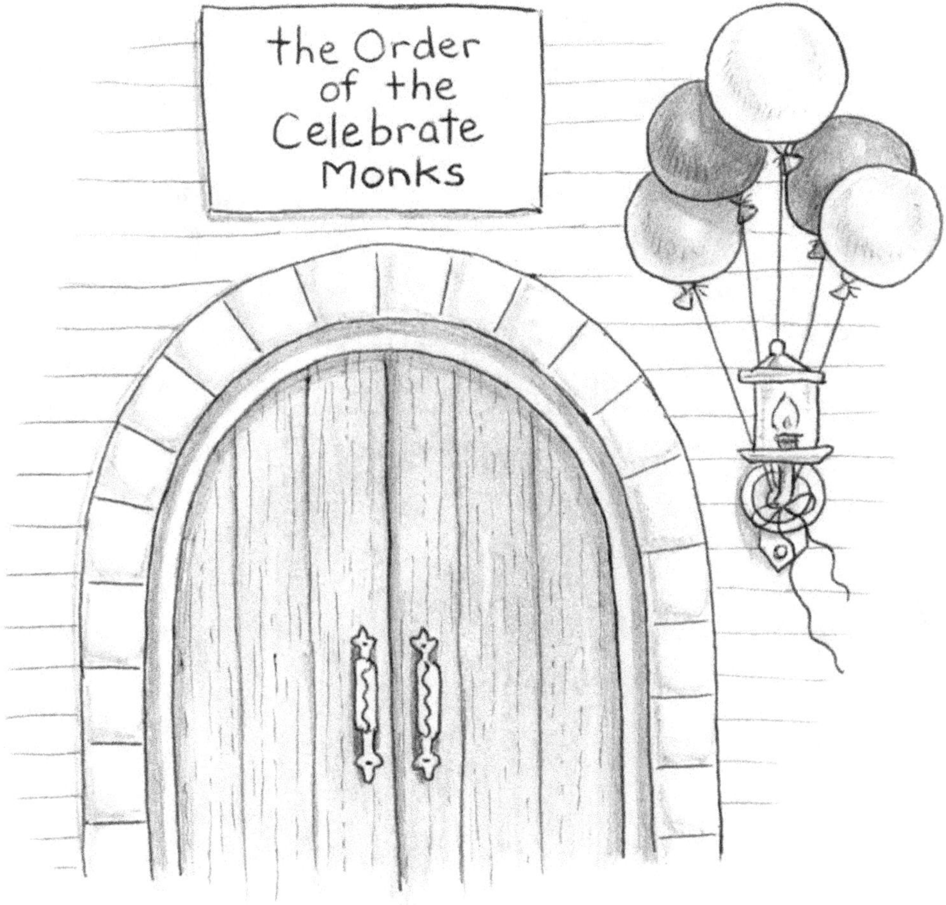
the Order
of the
Celebrate
Monks

God spelled
backwards
is still God

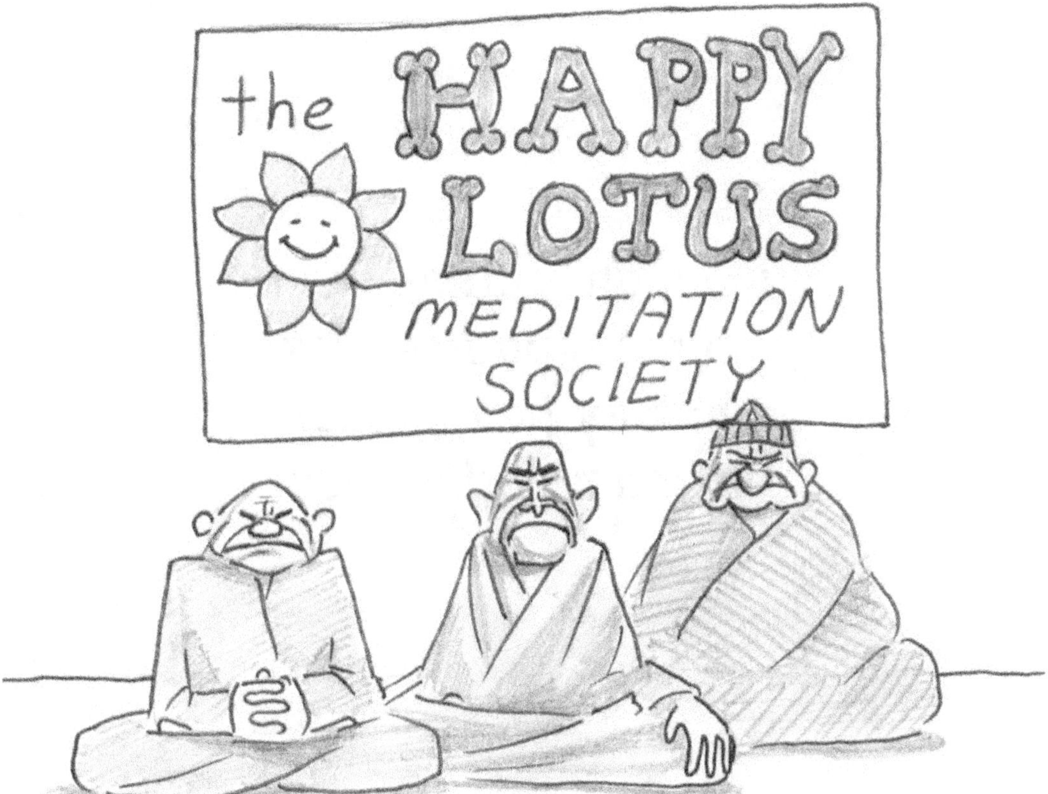
the HAPPY LOTUS
MEDITATION
SOCIETY

om mani padme hum
om mani padme hum
oh money pay me some
om mani padme hum

Truth is the alarm –

Grace is the snooze alarm

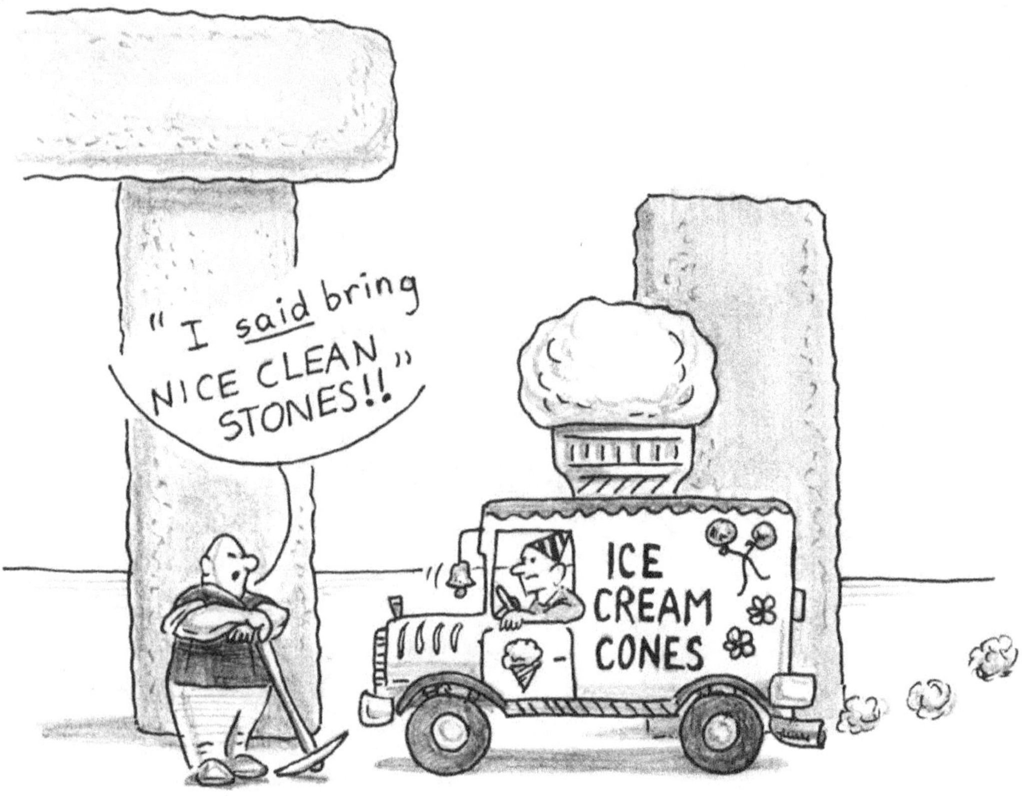
"I said bring NICE CLEAN STONES!!"
ICE CREAM CONES

the construction
of Stonehenge

I think I
just caught
your
Karma

self service
for Gas
selfless service
for God

the Sacred Order
of the
Extremely Large Hats

the Pharaoh Iminhotub IV

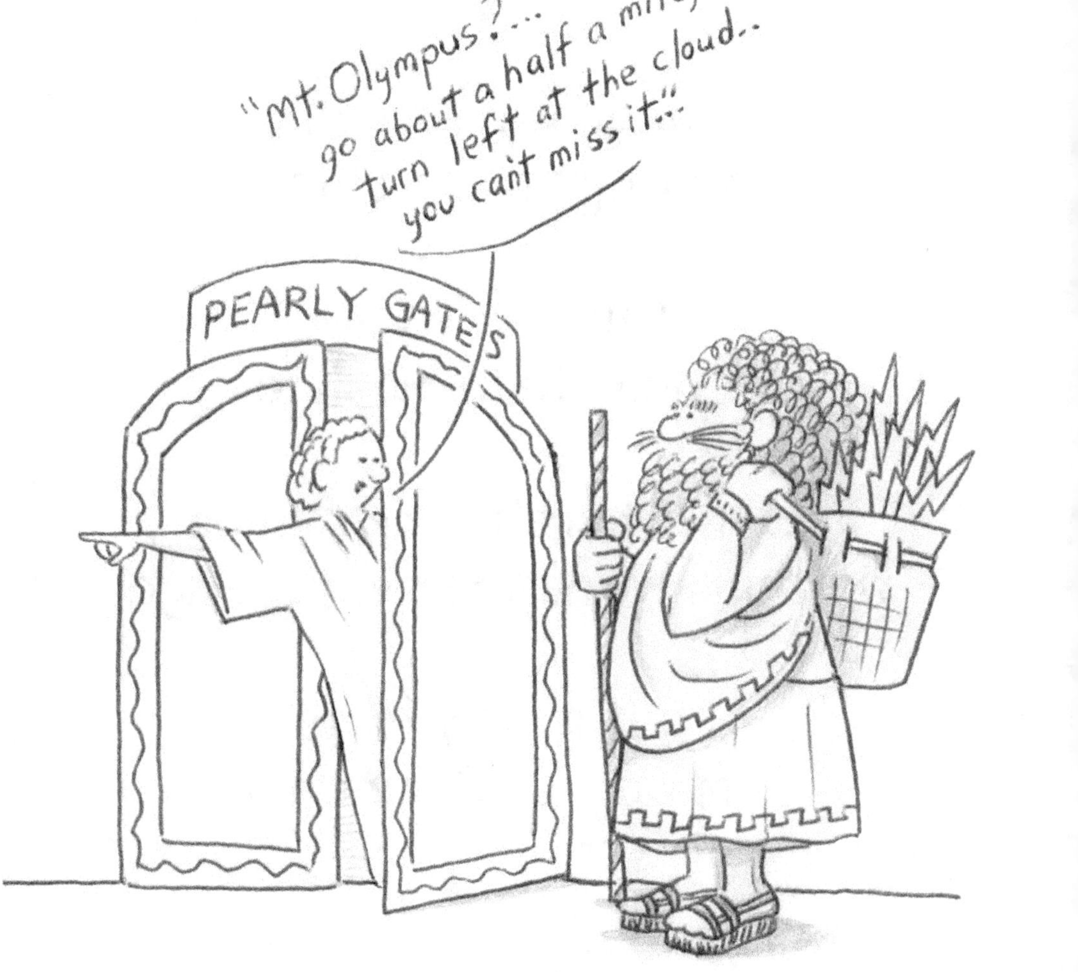
"Mt. Olympus?...
go about a half a mile,
turn left at the cloud..
you can't miss it.."
PEARLY GATES

when we're young
we want to be older -

when we're old
we want to be younger -

somewhere in the middle
we think we're the perfect age -

but it only lasts
for about 2 minutes

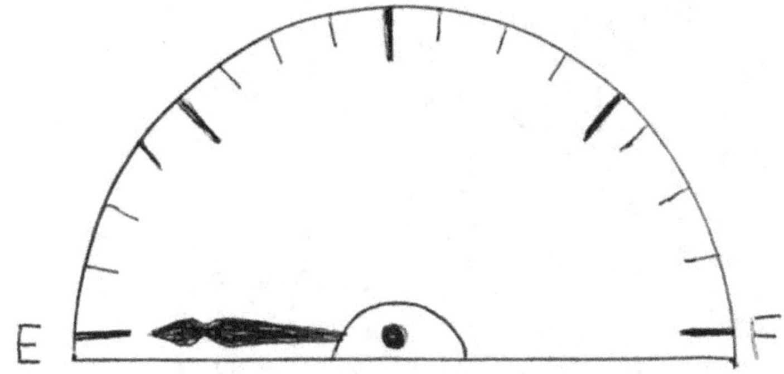
E
F

a mind runs better on empty

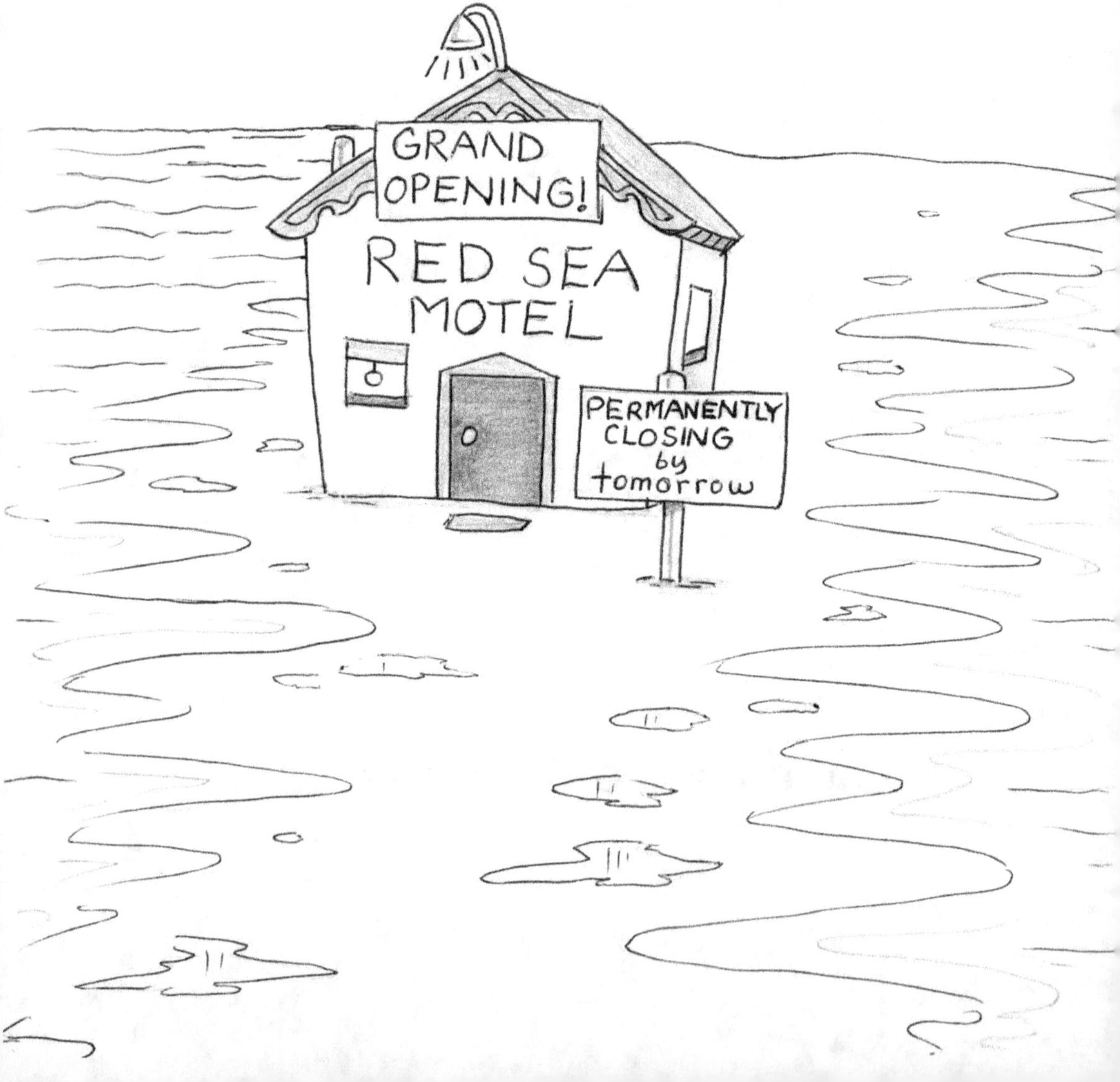
GRAND OPENING!
RED SEA MOTEL
PERMANENTLY CLOSING by tomorrow

glasses for
math class

glasses for
meditation class

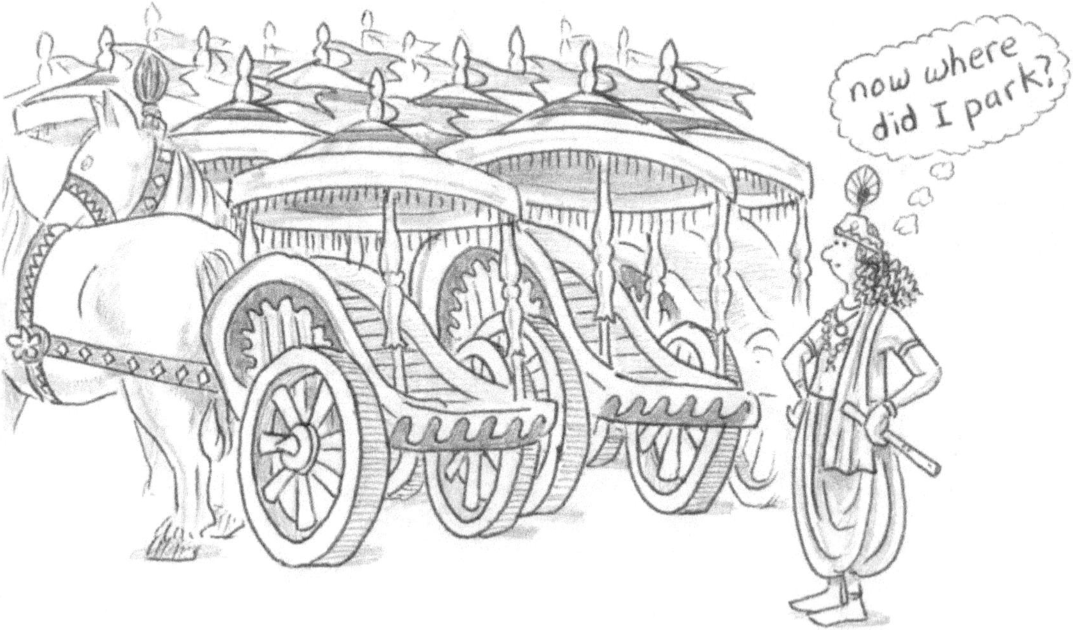
now where did I park?

Krishna, off to save the world!

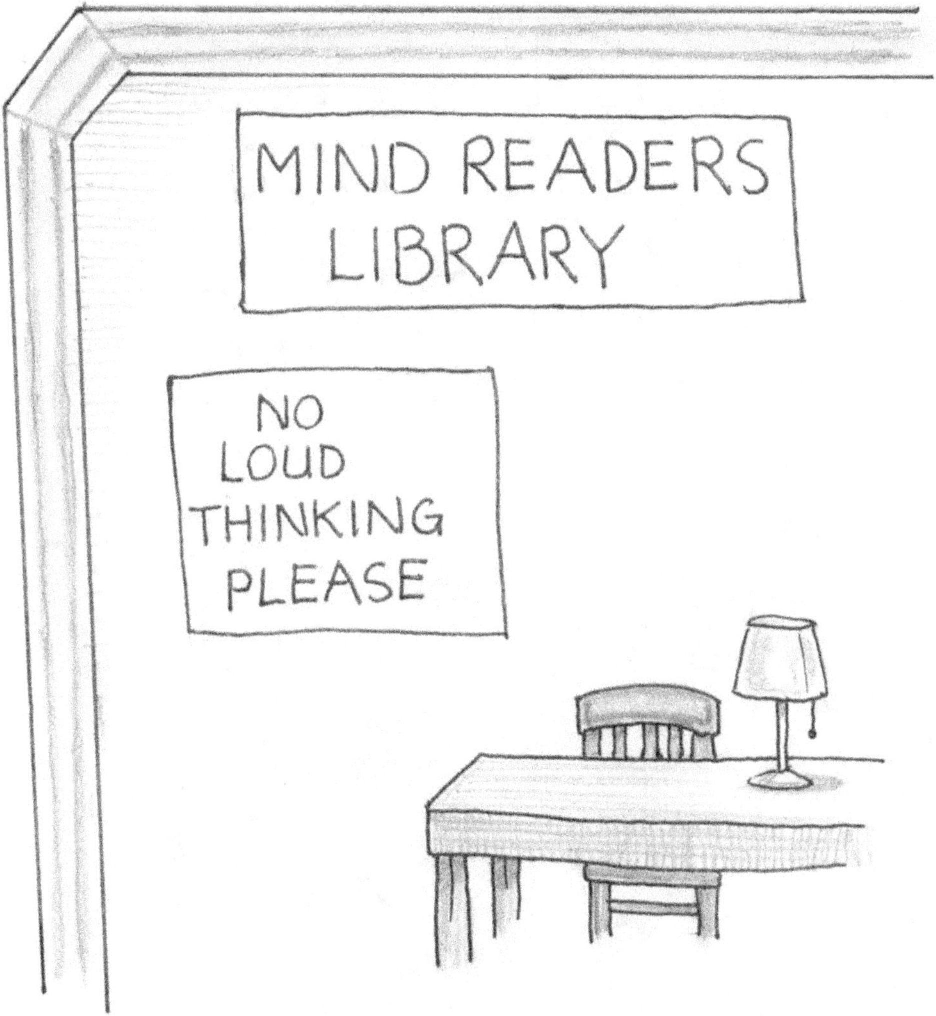
MIND READERS LIBRARY
NO LOUD THINKING PLEASE

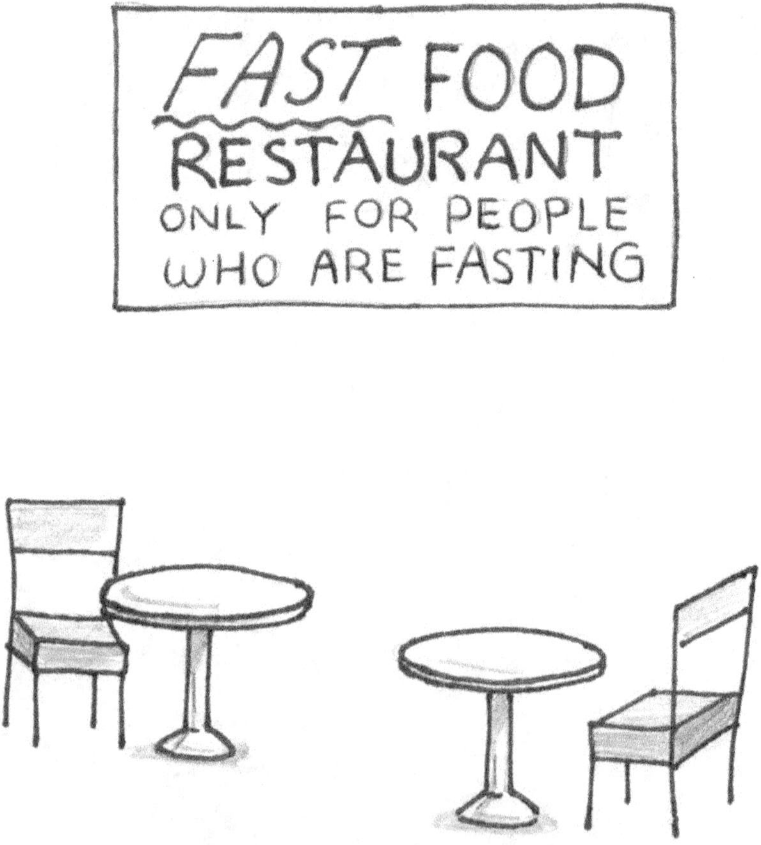
FAST FOOD
RESTAURANT
ONLY FOR PEOPLE
WHO ARE FASTING

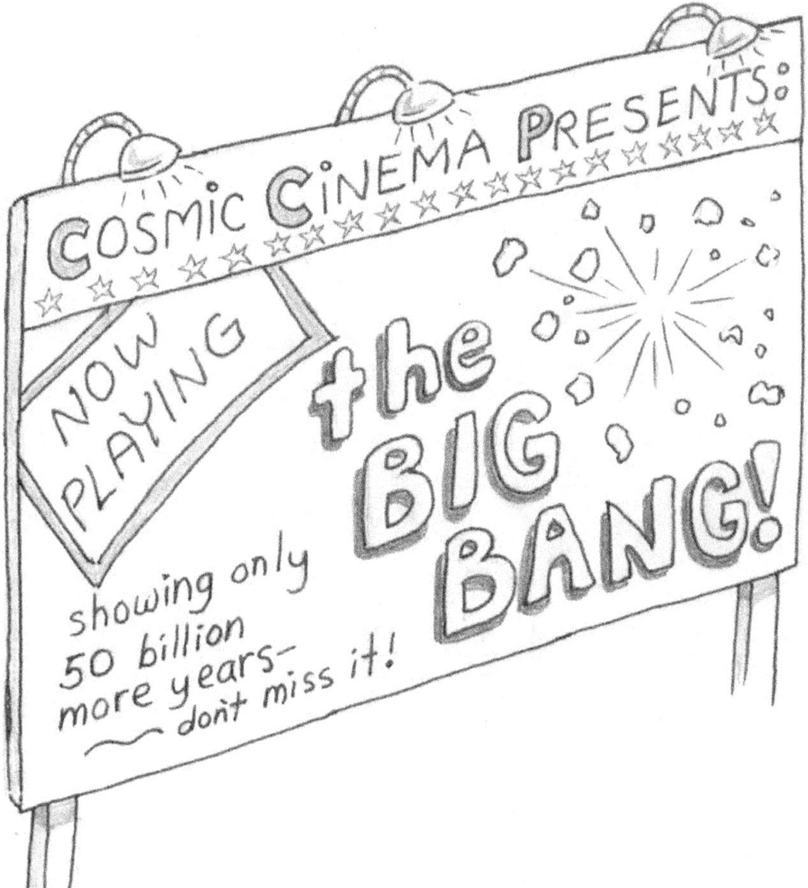
COSMIC CINEMA PRESENTS:
NOW PLAYING
the BIG BANG!
showing only 50 billion more years— don't miss it!

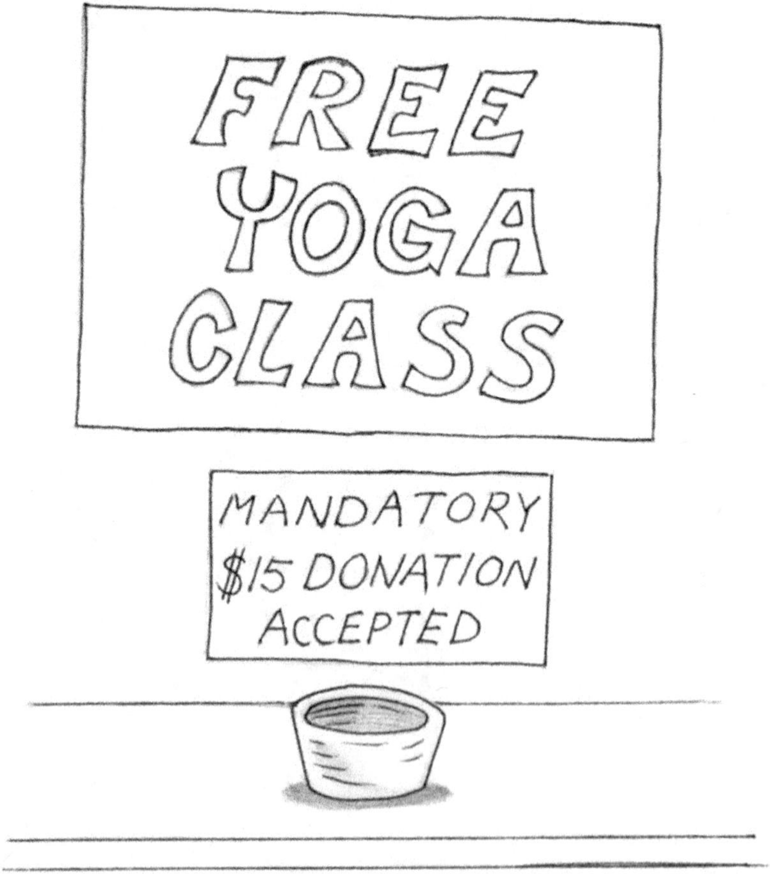
FREE YOGA CLASS
MANDATORY $15 DONATION ACCEPTED

change is good

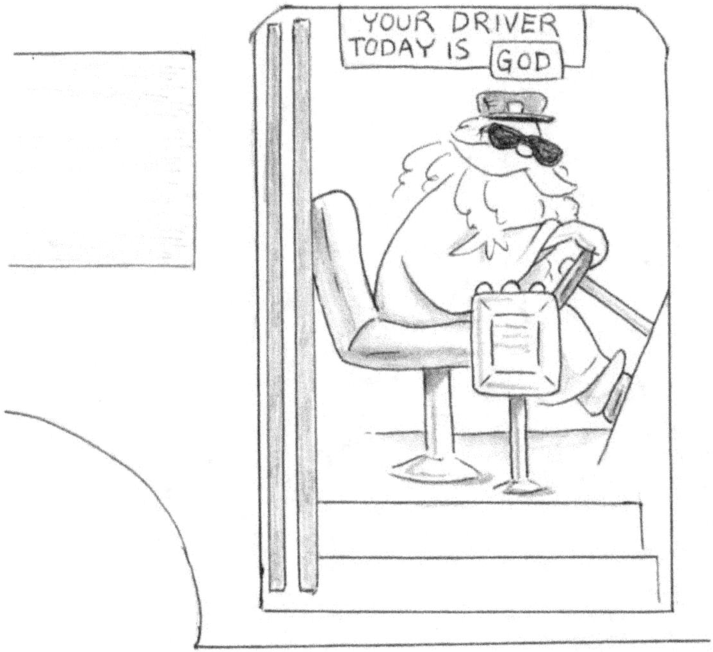
YOUR DRIVER TODAY IS
GOD

just be sure
you have the right change

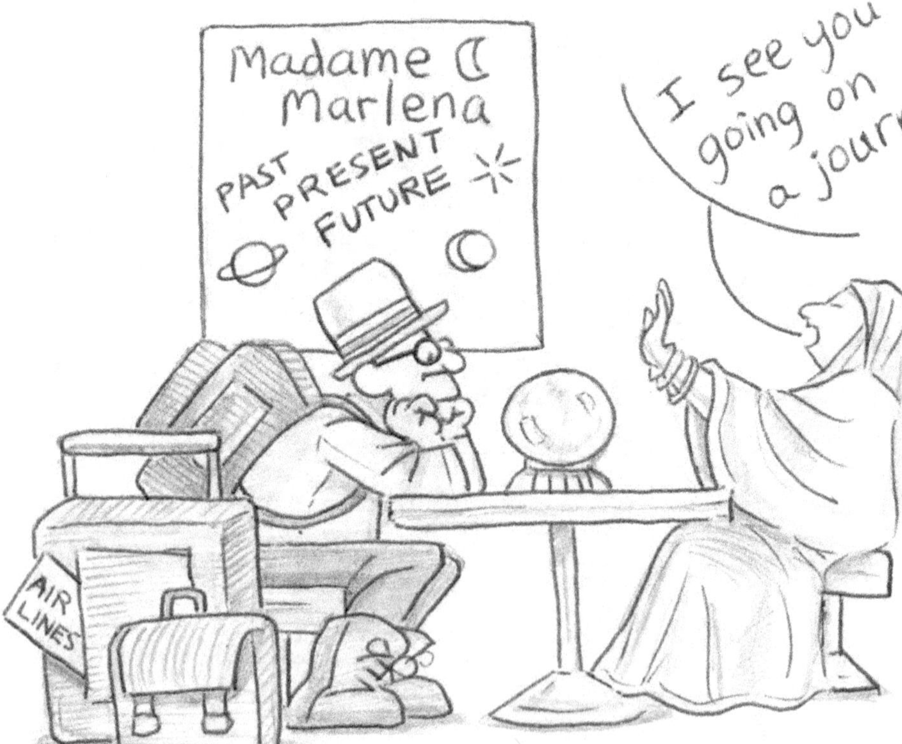
Madame Marlena
PAST PRESENT FUTURE
I see you going on a journey..
AIR LINES

Google
is God's nickname

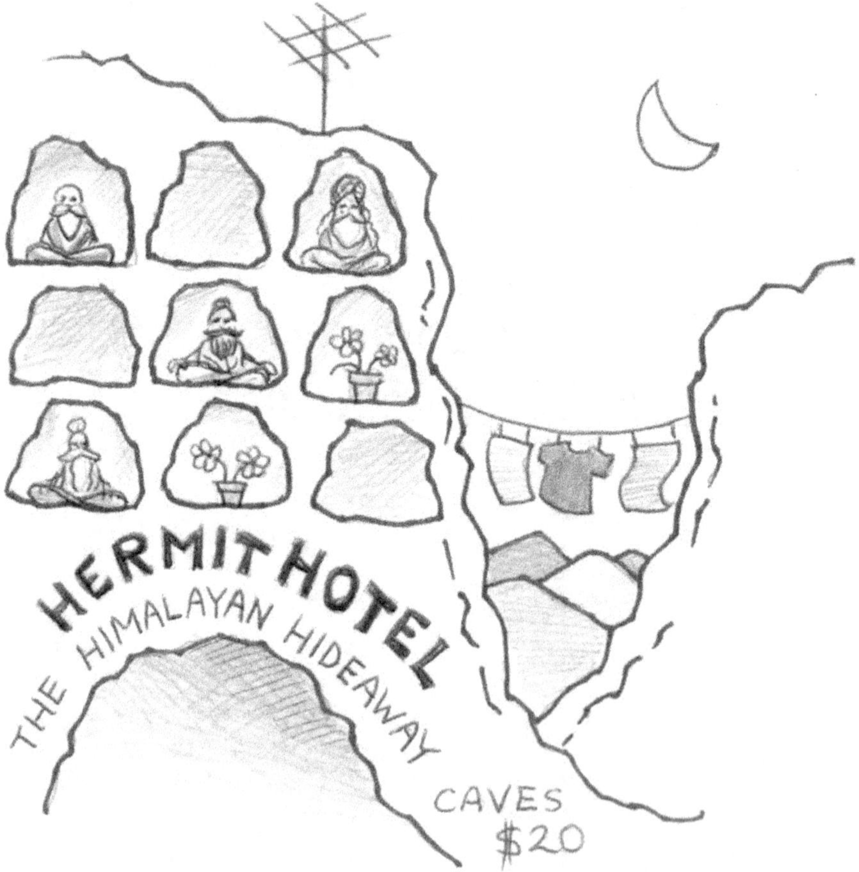
HERMIT HOTEL
THE HIMALAYAN HIDEAWAY
CAVES
$20

Love everything ~~except~~ yourself.
accept

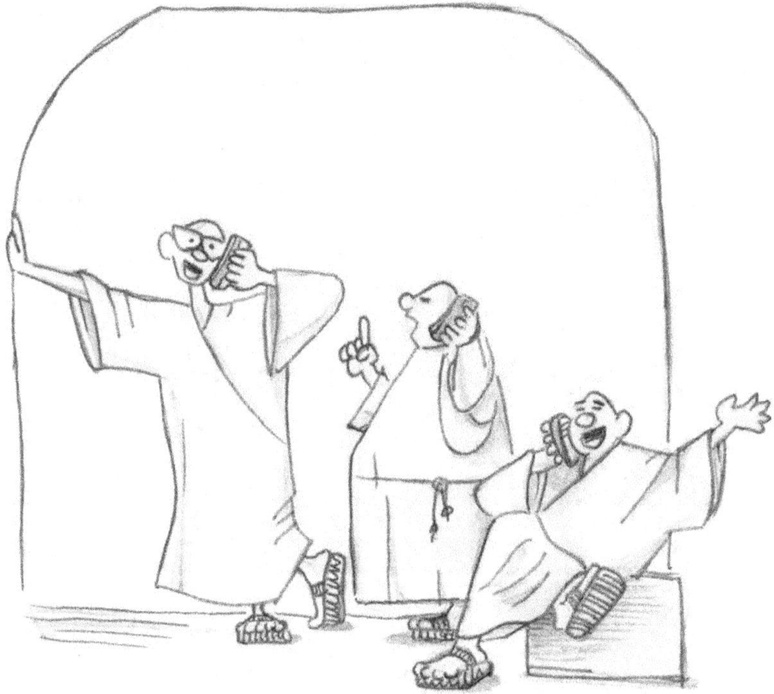

silent monks
10 minute talking break

to God
one plus one
is one

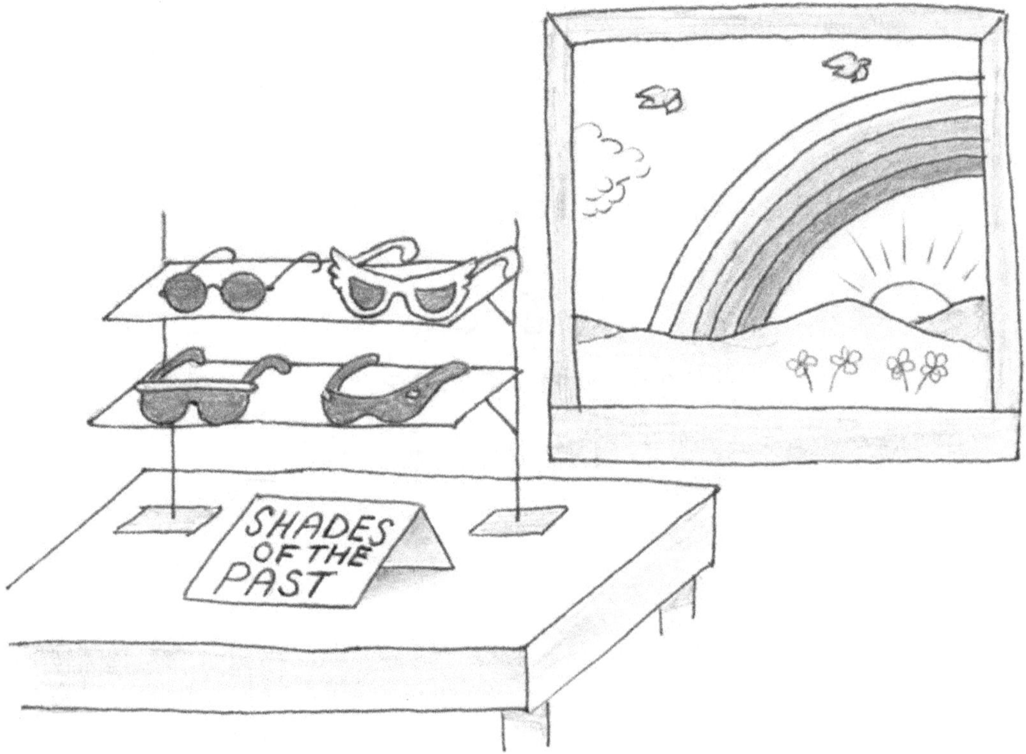
SHADES
OF THE
PAST

see the true colors

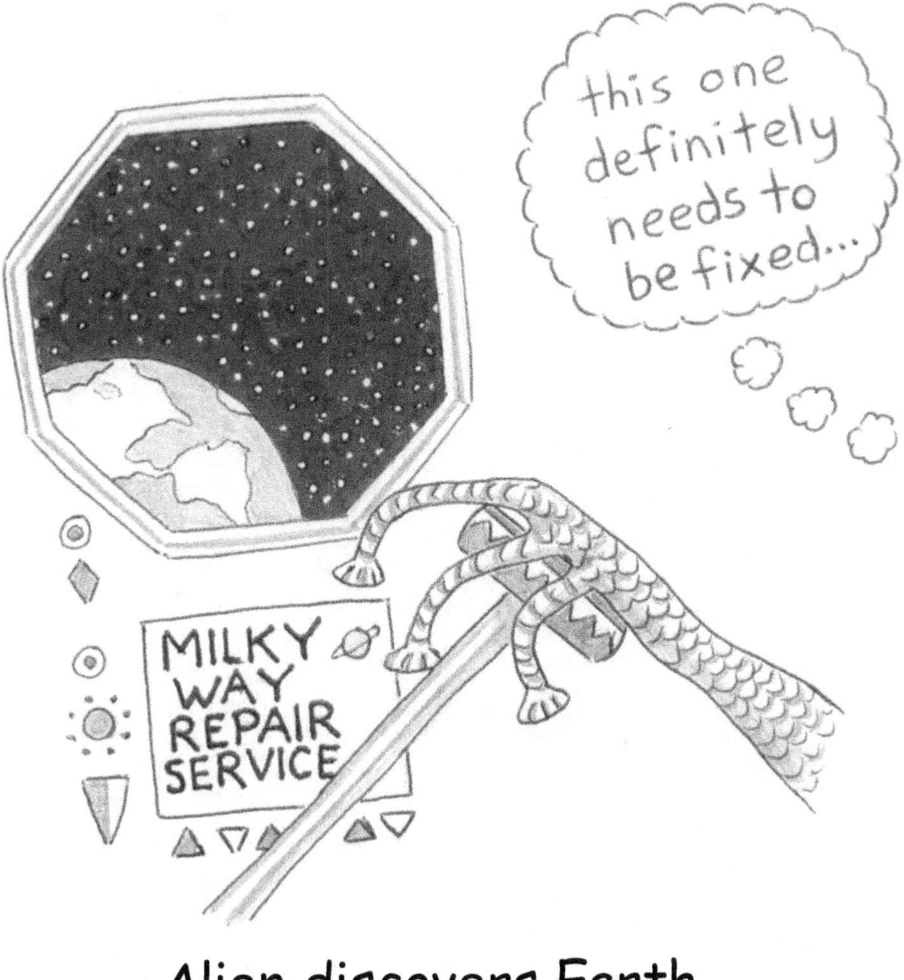
this one definitely needs to be fixed...
MILKY WAY REPAIR SERVICE

Alien discovers Earth

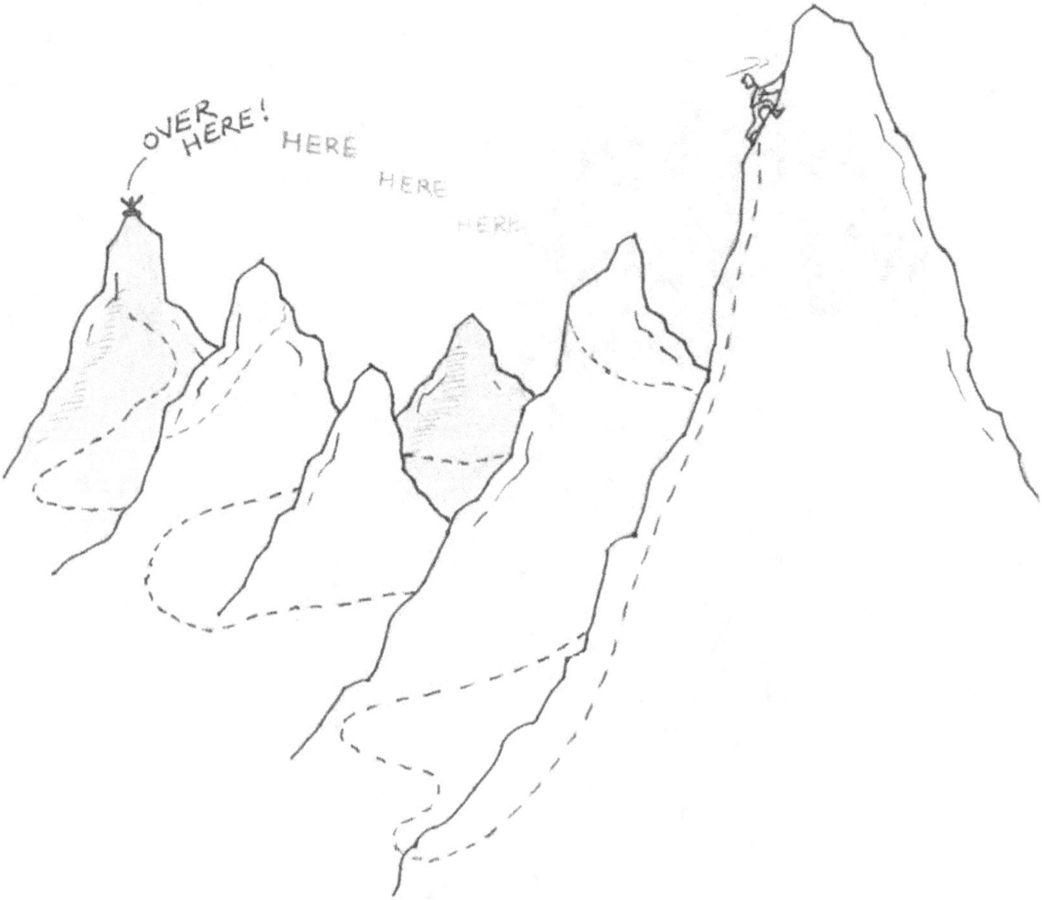
OVER HERE!
HERE
HERE
HERE

searching for the Guru

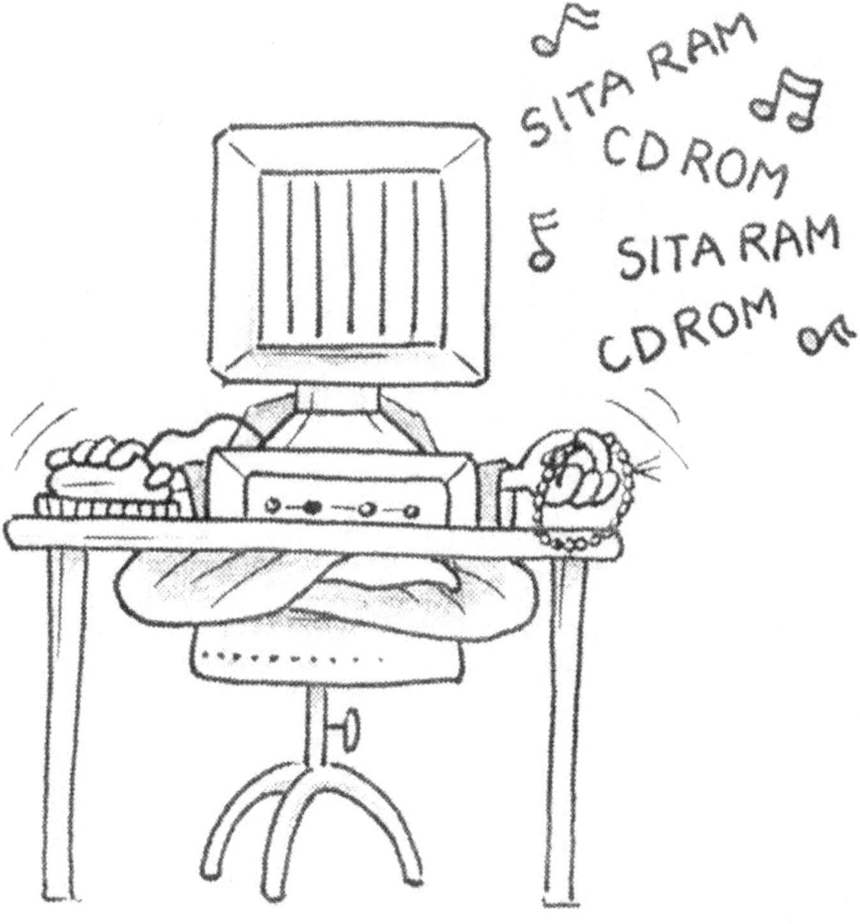
SITA RAM
CD ROM
SITA RAM
CD ROM

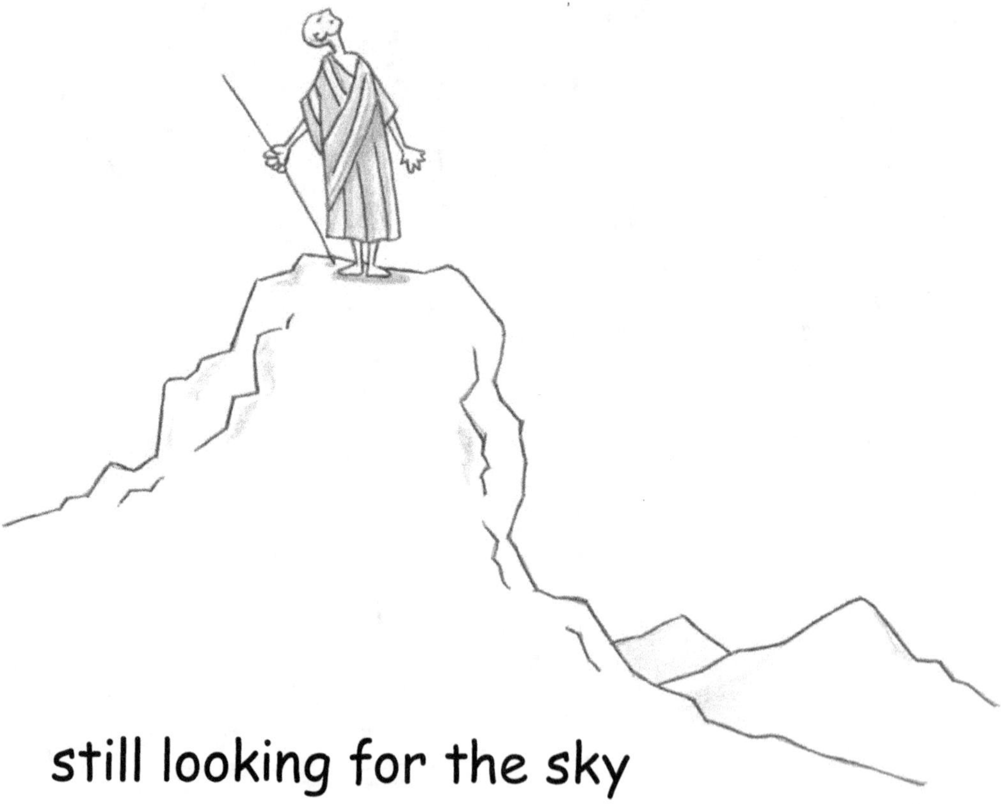

still looking for the sky

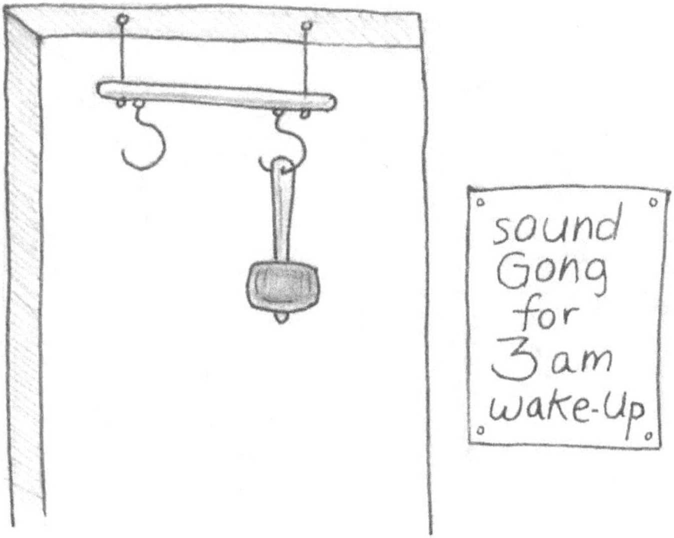
sound
Gong
for
3 am
wake-up

the monks sleep blissfully
until 10 am
ever since the mysterious
disappearance
of the temple gong

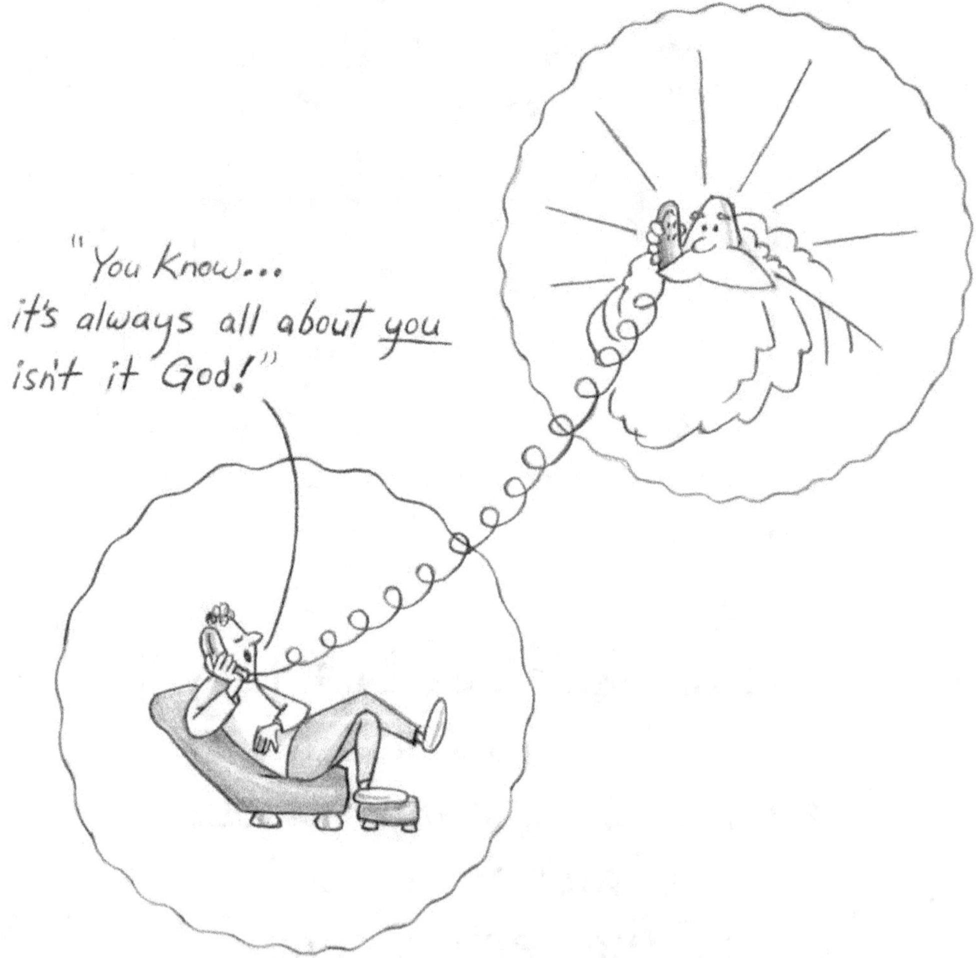
"You know...
it's always all about you
isn't it God!"

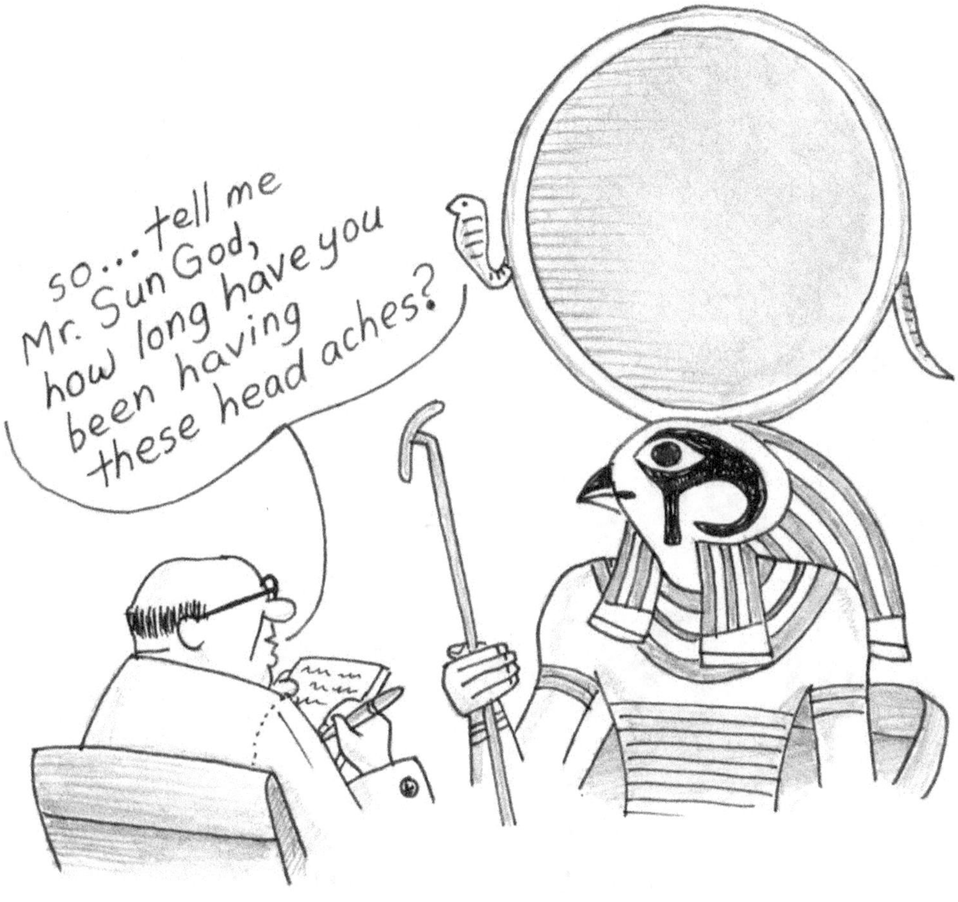
so... tell me Mr. Sun God, how long have you been having these head aches?

actual photo of
a Yogi levitating

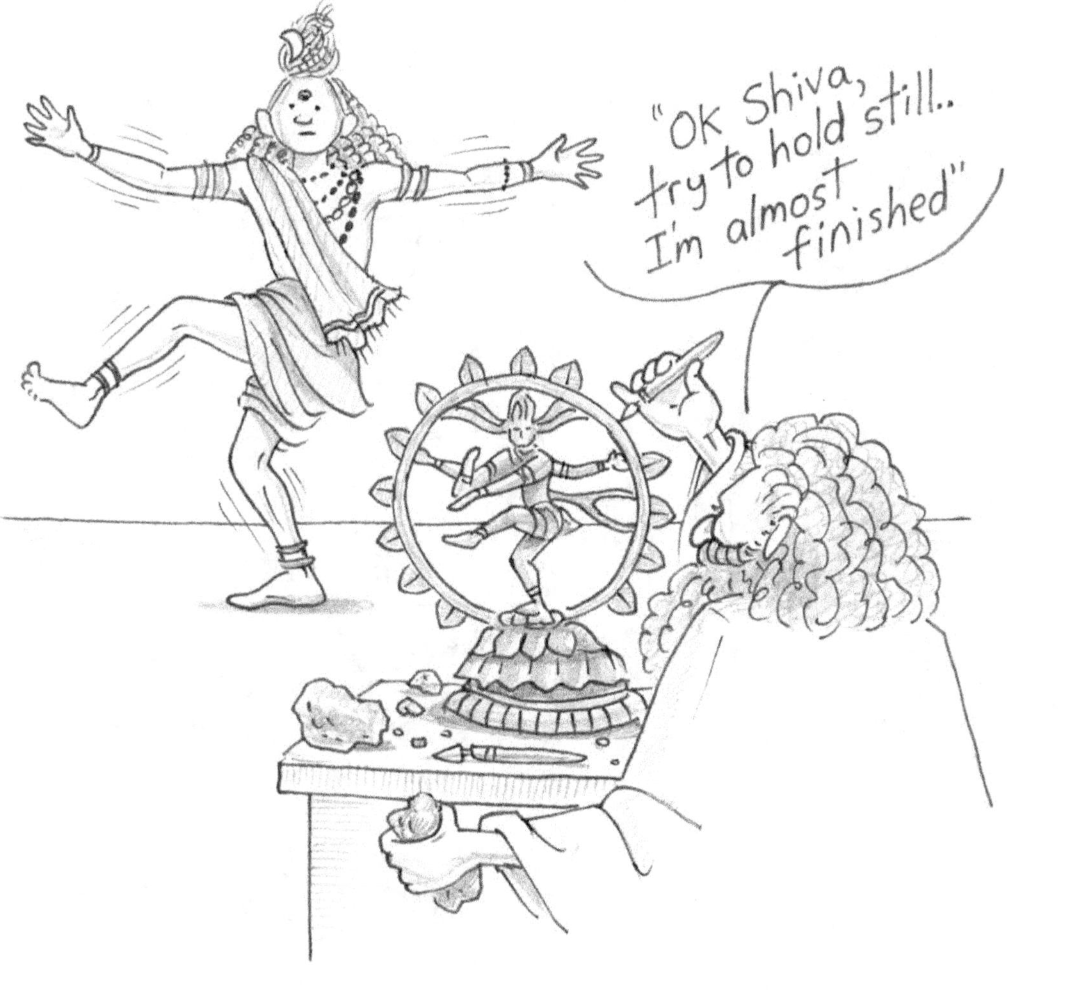
"Ok Shiva, try to hold still.. I'm almost finished"

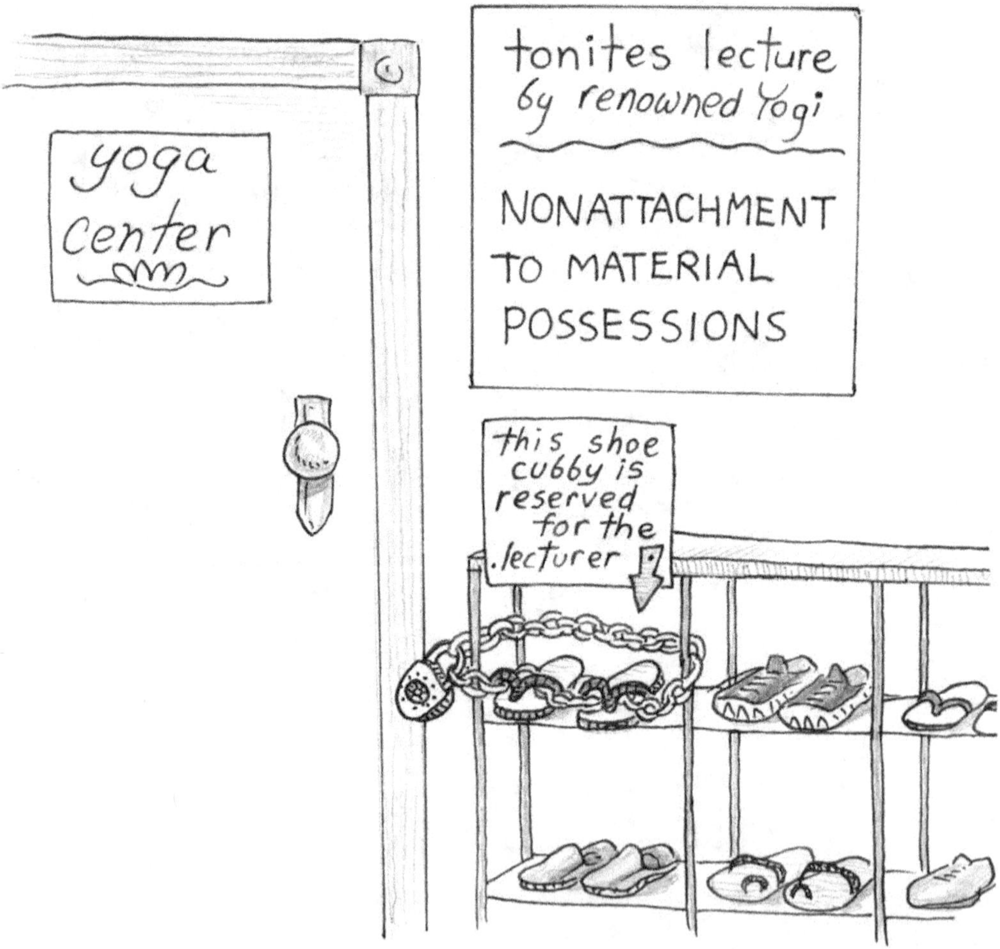
yoga center
tonites lecture by renowned Yogi
NONATTACHMENT TO MATERIAL POSSESSIONS
this shoe cubby is reserved for the lecturer

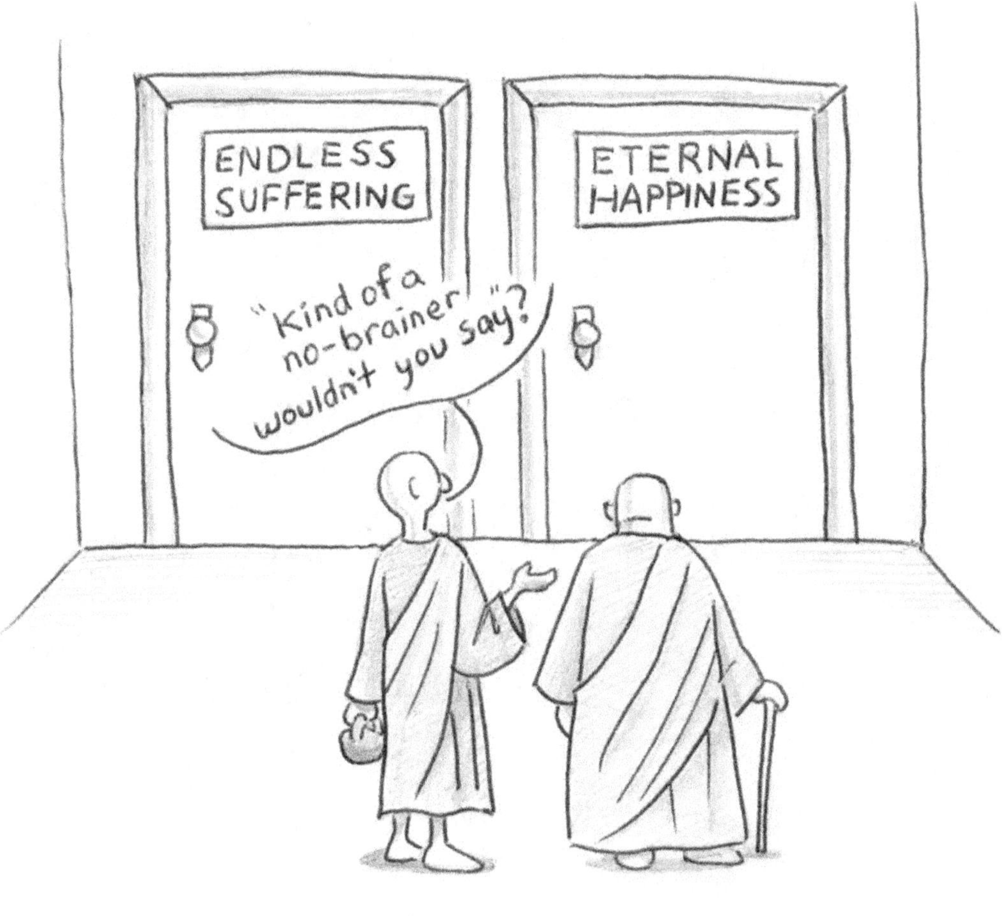
ENDLESS SUFFERING
ETERNAL HAPPINESS
"Kind of a no-brainer" wouldn't you say?

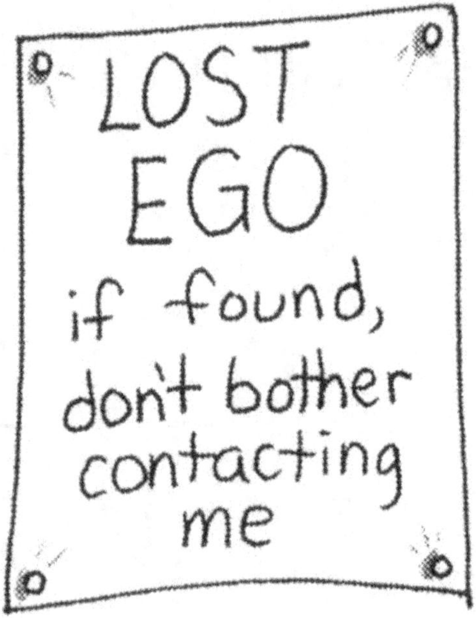
LOST
EGO
if found,
don't bother
contacting
me

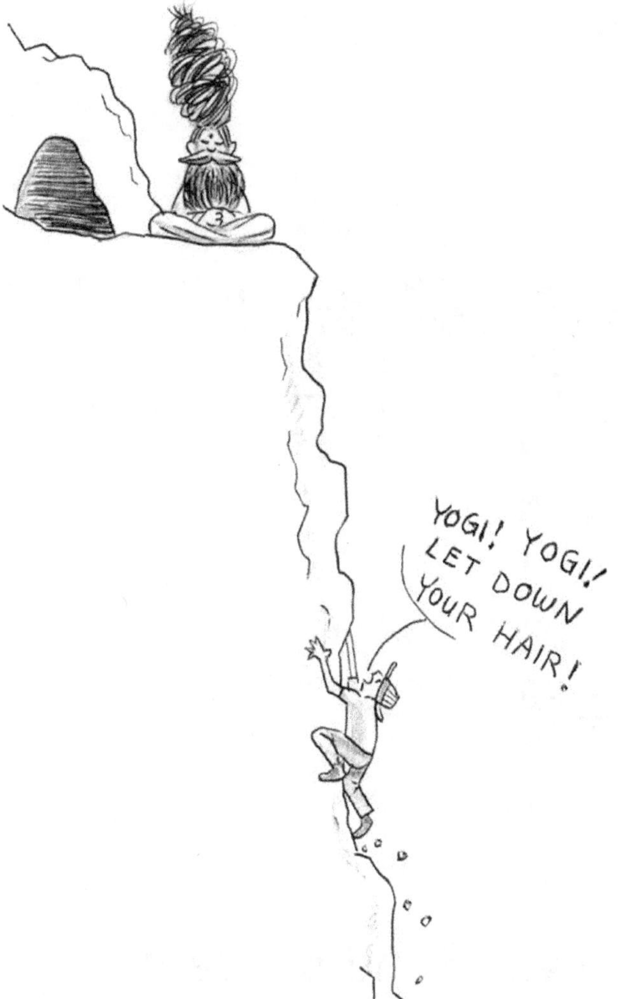
YOGI! YOGI! LET DOWN YOUR HAIR!

always live in the present

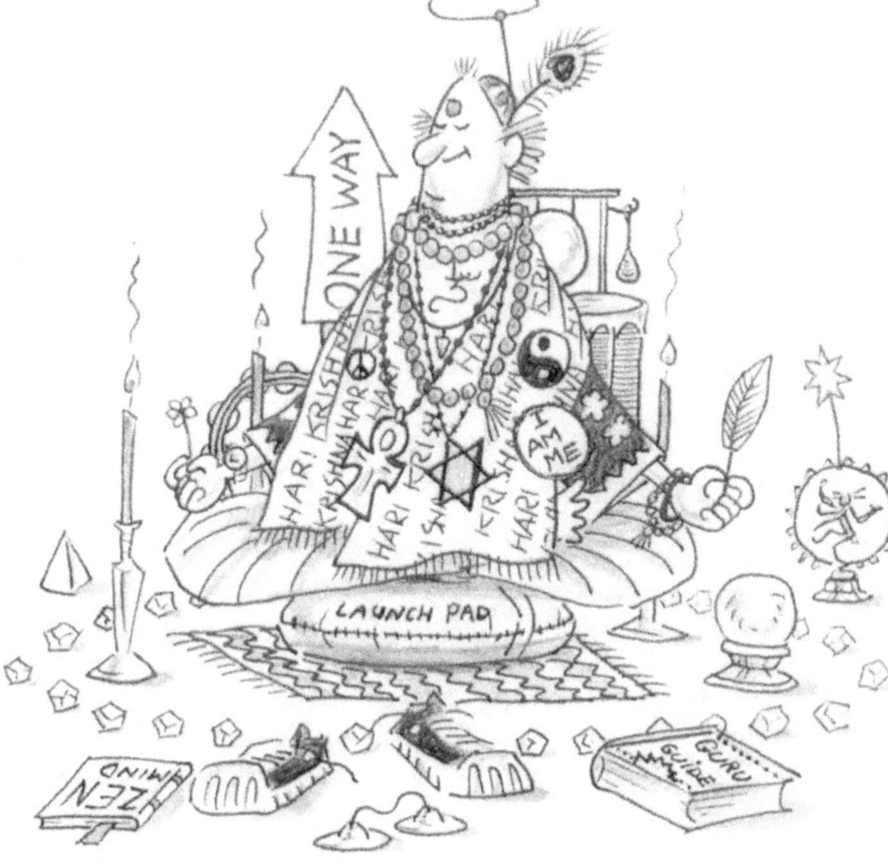
ONE WAY
I AM ME
LAUNCH PAD
ZEN MIND
GURU GUIDE

ok God... I'm ready!

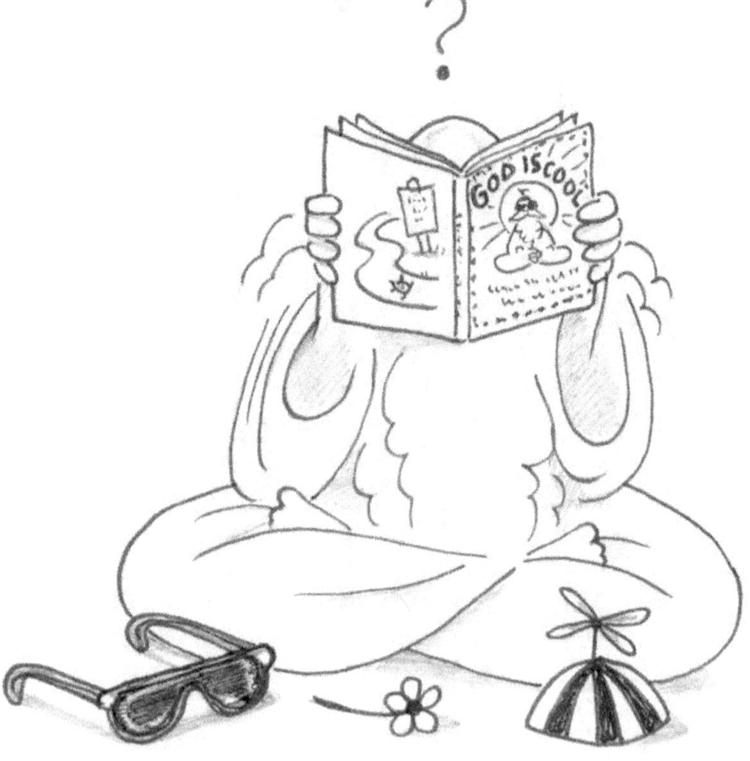
GOD IS COOL

Humor is very valuable...
without it,
everyone would be laughing
for no reason.

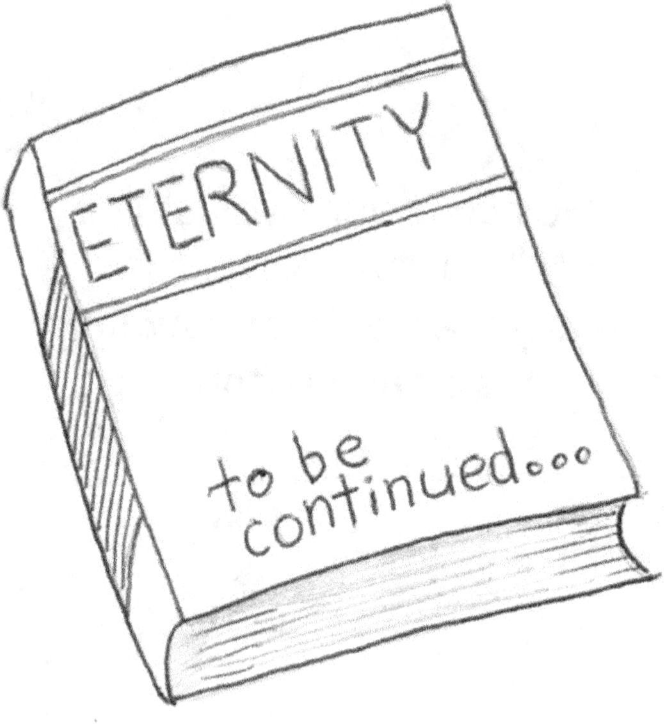
ETERNITY
to be continued...

www.ingramcontent.com/pod-product-compliance
Lightning Source LLC
Chambersburg PA
CBHW081359290426
44110CB00018B/2428